Allen W. Smith's explosive book, *The Looting of Social Security: How The Government Is Draining America's Retirement Account,* shocked many Americans when it was released by Carroll & Graf in January 2004. It exposed a little-known government practice that President Bush now routinely admits in his Social Security speeches. The government has been embezzling the Social Security surplus and spending it as if it were general fund revenue for the past 22 years!

ALA Booklist described *The Looting of Social Security* as "...a scathing account of massive fraud on the part of our nation's leaders, who have plundered every cent of the Social Security Trust Fund surplus that was specifically earmarked for the retirement of the baby boomers..."

The Boston Globe wrote: "With dismal clarity, Smith lays out the step-by-step history of how a national pension plan was transformed into an outright shakedown of working people...."

Social Security: The Attempt to Kill It is even more explosive. In addition to updating the looting fraud that is still taking place on a daily basis, Smith releases a new bombshell. In 1983, representatives of the Cato Institute and the Heritage Foundation developed a strategic long-term plan to destroy Social Security and replace it with private accounts. The plan was published in the Fall, 1983 edition of The Cato Journal with the title, "Achieving a Leninist Strategy."

The plan, which calls for waging "guerilla warfare against Social Security and its supporters," specifically sets out a game plan for replacing the current Social Security system with private accounts. This game plan is clearly the same one that President Bush is following as he tries to privatize Social Security.

ALSO BY ALLEN W. SMITH

The Looting of Social Security

*The Alleged Budget Surplus, Social Security &
Voodoo Economics*

Demystifying Economics

Understanding Economics

Understanding Inflation and Unemployment

SOCIAL SECURITY

The Attempt To Kill It

ALLEN W. SMITH, PH.D.

Author of

The Looting of Social Security

IRONWOOD PUBLICATIONS
Winter Haven, Florida

Library of Congress Control Number: 2005905023

ISBN 0-9648504-1-9

Printed in the United States of America

For my wife,

Joan Rugel Smith

and family

Mark, Jacki, Connor, and Noah

Michael and Dealyne

Lisa and Gary

Grandma, Inez W. Smith

CONTENTS

PREFACE

The current Social Security "crisis" was made in Washington. It has been 22 years in the making, and it is the handiwork of presidents and Congresses (both Republicans and Democrats), the Cato Institute, the Heritage Foundation, and many other individuals and organizations.

The actual solvency problem is not with the Social Security program. It is with the government's total budget. The 1983 payroll tax increase, enacted on the recommendation of the National Commission on Social Security, headed by Alan Greenspan, took care of the baby boomer problem. Taxes were raised high enough so that the baby-boom generation paid both the cost of the retirement of the generation that preceded them, as was customary, and also prepaid most of the cost of their own retirement, which was not customary. The 1983 tax increase generated $1.7 trillion in Social Security surplus between 1984 and 2005, and it will generate another $2 trillion between 2005 and 2017. This means that the Social Security trust fund should have $3.7 trillion in real assets in 2017, which would be enough to pay full Social Security benefits until 2041 when the youngest of the baby boomers will be 77 years old.

The problem is that the government did not save and invest the Social Security surplus as it was supposed to do. Instead it "borrowed" and spent (embezzled) every dollar of the Social Security surplus, replacing the money with worthless non-marketable special issue government IOUs. This means that Social Security will not have that $3.7 trillion reserve to help pay Social Security benefits between 2017 and 2041 unless the government pays back the looted money. The only way the government could repay the money is by passing hefty tax increases, borrowing massive additional amounts from the public, or cutting spending.

It would be bad enough if this were the only problem facing Social Security, but it is not. In 1983, the same year that Social Security was "fixed," members of the Cato Institute and the Heritage Foundation drew up a long-term plan for privatizing Social Security. They published their plan, entitled "Achieving A Leninist Strategy" in the Fall 1983 issue of *Cato Journal.* This plan served as the foundation upon which a powerful movement to destroy the current Social Security system and replace it with private accounts was built over the years.

The goal was to have a privatization plan waiting in the wings when the next Social Security crisis came along. Apparently the libertarians became impatient waiting for a true crisis to come and convinced President Bush to create an artificial crisis in the minds of the American public. Bush has done a good job of casting doubts on the long-term solvency of Social Security as part of the plan to privatize the program.

The real crisis is not about Social Security. The real crisis is a crisis of fraud and credibility with the United States government. A plot to destroy Social Security that was initially created by people at the Cato Institute and the Heritage Foundation now includes the participation of the President of the United States, many members of Congress, and many other conservative organizations.

My previous book, *The Looting of Social Security: How The Government Is Draining America's Retirement Account* (Carroll & Graf, 2004) covers the details of what happened to the Social Security surplus money that is supposed to be in the trust fund. This book picks up where that book left off. It exposes the 22-year-old plot to circumvent the American democratic process and build a strategy to dismantle the current Social Security system and replace it with private accounts despite the fact that the majority of Americans support the current system.

CHAPTER ONE

Introduction

...To make sure the retirement savings of America's seniors are not diverted in any other program, my budget protects all $2.6 trillion of the Social Security surplus for Social Security, and for Social Security alone.

--President George W. Bush, State of the Union Address, February 27, 2001

Federal Reserve Chairman, Alan Greenspan, launched a verbal bombshell, which set off a political storm, on February 25, 2004 when he proposed cutting Social Security benefits in testimony before the House Budget Committee. Social Security had not received much public attention since the "fix" of 1983, and most Americans believed that the program was fiscally sound. Thus, Greenspan's call for trimming benefits for future retirees touched a nerve in many Americans, especially those nearing retirement.

Greenspan said, "We are over-committed at this stage. It is important that we tell people who are about to retire what it is they will have." He warned that the government should not "promise more than we are able to deliver."

Greenspan pointed to the forthcoming retirement of the baby-boom generation as the reason for his concern. He said, "This dramatic demographic change is certain to place enormous demands on our nation's resources—demands we will almost surely be unable to meet unless action is taken. For a variety of reasons, that action is better taken as soon as possible."

Few people knew it at the time, but Greenspan's February 25, 2004 statement was the opening salvo in an organized campaign to dismantle Social Security, as we now know it. Six months later, on August 27, 2004, Greenspan again spoke of cutting Social Security benefits during remarks at a symposium in Jackson Hole, Wyoming.

"As a nation, we owe it to our retirees to promise only the benefits that can be delivered," Greenspan said. "If we have promised more than our economy has the ability to deliver to retirees without unduly diminishing real income gains of workers, as I fear we may have, we must recalibrate our public programs so that pending retirees have time to adjust through other channels."

Just like his February statement, this new statement on Social Security by the Fed Chairman generated a lot of headlines and news coverage. An article by Nell Henderson in the August 27, 2004 edition of the Washington Post carried the headline,

"Greenspan Urges Pension Benefit Cuts." The idea that Social Security might be in some kind of long-term financial trouble began to sink in. When Alan Greenspan speaks, America listens, so the notion of a problem with Social Security financing could not be totally ignored when a man of Greenspan's stature suggested there was a problem.

Social Security observers began to focus on the 2004 presidential election campaign to see if President Bush made an issue of Social Security. He made a brief reference to privatization in his acceptance speech at the convention. He said, "In an ownership society, more people will own their health care plans, and have the confidence of owning a piece of their retirement. We'll always keep the promise of Social Security for our older workers. With the huge Baby Boom generation approaching retirement, many of our children and grandchildren understandably worry whether Social Security will be there when they need it. We must strengthen Social Security by allowing younger workers to save some of their taxes in a personal account—a nest egg you can call your own, and government can never take away."

Bush made occasional reference to his "ownership society" and private Social Security accounts during the fall campaign, but he never made them a major issue. He certainly didn't suggest during the campaign that Social Security was facing an imminent crisis. How could he? He had been president for the past four years and had made no effort to reform Social Security, so there would not have been many votes to gain by trying to scare people into believing that Social Security was in deep trouble during the campaign. Social Security as a campaign issue was dwarfed by his proposal for a Constitutional Amendment prohibiting same-sex marriages.

Once Bush was re-elected and no longer had to worry about the voters, Social Security reform suddenly rushed to the top of his domestic agenda. At a press conference on November 4, 2004, Bush said, "Let me put it to you this way: I earned capital in the campaign, political capital, and now I intend to spend it. It is my style...I've earned capital in this election—and I'm going to spend it for what I told the people I'd spend it on, which is—you've heard the agenda: Social Security and tax reform, moving this economy forward, education, fighting and winning the war on terror."

Bush then began traveling around the country making his Social Security pitch to carefully screened audiences. Unlike FDR's famous statement about fear, "The only thing we have to fear is fear itself," Bush began trying to instill fear over Social Security's solvency in every American. He used scare tactics and all the powers of persuasion that he possessed to try to convince the public that Social Security was facing a crisis and that at least part of the solution was to use Social Security revenue to fund individual private account.

The approach Bush was advocating would weaken Social Security—not strengthen it. So what was the president trying to accomplish? He was trying to drive a large nail into the coffin of Social Security as the first step toward dismantling it. Conservatives have hated Social Security since the day it passed under Franklin D. Roosevelt in 1935, and they have been trying to destroy it ever since. George W. Bush would love to leave the legacy of being the president who got rid of Social Security, and he is determined to do so by blaming it all on the baby boom generation.

The baby boomers, who have been blamed for almost every social problem that has arisen since their birth (1946-1964), became the victims of a plot designed to blame them for the alleged Social Security crisis and to cheat them out of benefits for which they have already paid. The attempted rip-off began with Alan Greenspan's call for cuts in Social Security benefits. Up until that time most Americans were unaware that Social Security was facing any serious financial problems, either short-term or long-term. After all, President George W. Bush was in the fourth year of his first term, and he had barely talked about Social Security. He was the tax-cut president who had argued repeatedly that our economy was strong, and government finances were so good that we should return some of the money to the public through massive income tax cuts.

Federal Reserve Chairman, Alan Greenspan, should have known better than most just how solvent Social Security was. The 1983 payroll tax increase, enacted upon the recommendation of the National Commission on Social Security, headed by Greenspan, had allegedly "fixed" the baby boomer problem with regard to Social Security. That law required the baby boomers to pay enough taxes to fund the benefits of current retirees, plus enough additional taxes to prepay most of the cost of their own Social Security benefits. The additional tax revenue was supposed to go into the Social Security Trust Fund to build up a large reserve earmarked specifically for the retirement of the baby boomers. This reserve would be used to supplement the payroll tax revenue so that full benefits could be paid throughout the period of the boomers' retirement years without placing a disproportionate burden on the younger generation.

The 1983 legislation marked a sharp break with the traditional pay-as-you-go approach to funding Social Security benefits. After 1983, the Social Security system no longer operated on a strictly pay-as-you-go basis. For the baby-boom generation, Social Security has operated on a combination "pay-as-you-go" and "prepay-your-own-benefits" principle. Therefore, by the time the baby boomers retire, they will have prepaid a major portion of the entire cost of their benefits, as well as having funded the retirement benefits of retirees during the years between 1983 and their own retirement.

Despite the fact that Greenspan knew the baby boomers had prepaid the cost of their retirement, he silently watched both Republicans and Democrats misuse the money that was supposed to be going into the Social Security reserve without once alerting the public to the fraudulent activity. Because of the looting of the surplus money, the government will be unable to pay full Social Security benefits after 2017 without a tax increase to repay the looted funds. Therefore, Greenspan and Bush are proposing cheating the approximately 77 million baby boomers out of part of the benefits that they have already prepaid. At the same time, they are both supporting making the unaffordable Bush tax cuts permanent.

At the time that my book, *The Looting of Social Security: How The Government is Draining America's Retirement Program*, was published in January 2004, most Americans believed that their Social Security contributions went into a special trust fund where it accumulated, and then when they retired the money would be paid back to them out of the trust fund. The notion that the government was spending the surplus Social Security contributions, that were being paid in by the baby boomers in order to prepay the cost of their own retirement, to fund Bush's income tax cuts and for other government programs, was unthinkable in the minds of most Americans. Surely, our government would not take revenue that was collected specifically for Social Security and spend it on other programs.

This would be like using Grandma's retirement fund to pay current expenses because Grandma won't need the money until she actually retires. Any individual, who would drain the retirement fund of his or her grandmother without telling her, and without making any provisions for repayment of the funds when Grandma reached retirement age and needed the money, would be branded a scoundrel and a criminal. Yet, that is exactly what the United States Government has been doing since 1984.

The revenue from the Social Security payroll tax, earmarked exclusively for the payment of Social Security benefits, is routinely deposited into the general fund and all money that is not needed to pay for current benefits is spent as if it were general revenue. This is fraudulent, and it is a violation of Section 13301 of the Budget Enforcement Act of 1990, which explicitly prohibits co-mingling Social Security funds with general revenue funds.

Prior to the 1983 Social Security legislation, which increased payroll taxes for the explicit purpose of building up a large reserve in preparation for the retirement of the baby boomers, there had never been any significant Social Security surplus. In fact, Social Security ran small deficits for seven years in a row from 1976 to 1982. However, upon the recommendation of the Greenspan Commission, a substantial hike in the payroll tax was enacted into law.

This money was to have been saved and invested in order to build up a large reserve with which to fund the retirement of the baby boomers. By 2017 this tax increase will have generated approximately $3.7 trillion in surplus Social Security revenue. This would be enough to pay full benefits until at least 2041 if the money were actually in the trust fund as it is supposed to be.

The government of the United States has raided the trust fund on a regular basis for more than two decades and spent the surplus money on other government programs. So far, the tax increase has generated $1.7 trillion in surplus revenue, and it is expected to generate another $2.0 trillion between 2005 and 2017. Even as President Bush travels around the country claiming that he wants to "save" and "strengthen" Social Security, he continues to bleed the program to death. More than $400 million of Social Security surplus revenue is spent on other government programs each and every day.

I first discovered this fraudulent government practice while doing research in early 2000 for a previous book, "The Alleged Budget Surplus, Social Security, and Voodoo Economics." At first, I couldn't believe my findings. The elected officials of the United States government surely would not spend the Social Security contributions of American workers on other government programs without either their knowledge or permission. But the more I researched the subject the clearer it became that the government had done, and was continuing to do, exactly that.

I was outraged, and I wanted to tell the whole world so they would be outraged too. But nobody would listen. It just didn't seem credible that our own government, both Democrats and Republicans, would engage in such fraud against the American people. On September 27, 2000, I appeared on CNN with Lou Waters to discuss my newly published book. When I tried to explain that there was really no significant budget surplus except for the Social Security surplus and told Waters that the government was using Social Security money for other programs, he looked at me in disbelief.

"We're not hearing any of this in the news," Waters said. "I'm involved in the news. Are you a voice crying in the wilderness? And if not, why haven't we seen a presidential candidate, any presidential candidate, talk about this?"

I continued to be a voice crying in the wilderness for the next four years. I tried my heart out to alert the American public to the fact that, despite his pledge in the 2000 campaign to not use the Social Security surplus for anything except the payment of benefits, Bush was continuing to raid the trust fund, and that he was paying for his income tax cuts with Social Security money paid in the form of payroll taxes by working Americans.

It was a tough sell. It would probably have been easier for me to convince the news media and the public that I had taken a ride in a UFO than to convince them that Bush was spending every dollar of the Social Security surplus in violation of both his promise to the American people and in violation of federal law.

In early 2000, as part of my efforts to alert the public to the fact that the trust fund was being looted, I began sending material to candidate Al Gore. I sent him advance copies of my book, research findings, and several letters. I urged Gore to put distance between himself and Clinton on Social Security and take a stand against the continued use of Social Security money for non-Social Security purposes.

I used multiple channels in sending the material to Gore in order to be sure that some of it got to him. I even made phone calls on the eve of the convention to people who had direct access to Gore, urging them to bring the trust fund raiding to his attention.

Of course, I cannot be sure that I was the source of Gore's idea to propose the Social Security lockbox, and to make the raiding of the trust fund a major campaign issue. The important point is that Gore took a stand against continued raiding of the trust fund, which resulted in George W. Bush taking a similar stand.

In addition to promising many times during the campaign that he would not raid the Social Security trust fund, George W. Bush made additional pledges after he was sworn in as President. In his first State of the Union address, delivered on February 27, 2001, Bush said, *"To make sure the retirement savings of America's seniors are not diverted in any other program, my budget protects all $2.6 trillion of the Social Security surplus for Social Security, and for Social Security alone."*

Four days later in his national radio address to the American people, Bush said, *"We're going to keep the promise of Social Security and keep the government from raiding the Social Security surplus."*

There was nothing vague or conditional about these promises. The President of the United States had stated unequivocally that he would not spend the Social Security surplus. The American people like to think they can trust the word of their president, and so naturally they continued to believe throughout Bush's first term that the Social Security money was being protected. Although I continued to point out in radio interviews, op-ed articles, and by any other available means, that President Bush was spending the Social Security money despite his promise not to do so, almost nobody would take the word of an economist and writer over that of the President of the United States.

Since more than $500 billion in Social Security surplus flowed in during George W. Bush's first term, almost everybody felt certain that there was at least that much money in the trust fund, no matter what had happened under previous presidents. I could think of no way to convince the public that Bush was spending the Social Security money, although that was the basic premise of my 2004 book, "The Looting of Social Security."

I was fortunate to have the opportunity to appear on CNBC on February 26, 2004, the morning after Greenspan's first assault on Social Security was launched. I also had the opportunity to discuss my views on CNNfn and more than 100 live radio interviews, but still the public would not buy the notion that Bush was spending their Social Security surplus. I desperately needed to have a high profile credible person confirm what I had been saying for four years—that all Social Security surplus was being spent.

Not in my wildest imagination could I have dreamed that the person who would confirm Bush's ongoing spending of Social Security money would be Bush himself. Yet, that is exactly what happened.

On Wednesday February 9, 2005 President Bush, speaking at an event that was not even supposed to be about Social Security shocked many observers, including myself, when he openly admitted that surplus Social Security revenue generated by the payroll tax is spent on other government programs. I was even more shocked that the White House Press Office did not delete the Social Security remarks before issuing a news release with the title "Remarks by President Bush in a Conversation on Class-Action Reform."

President Bush's exact words as quoted in the news release issued by the White House Press Office follow.

Some in our country think that Social Security is a trust fund – in other words, there's a pile of money being accumulated. That's just simply not true. The money -- payroll taxes going into the Social Security are spent. They're spent on benefits and they're spent on government programs. There is no trust. We're on the ultimate pay-as-you-go system -- what goes in comes out. And so, starting in 2018, what's going in -- what's coming out is greater than what's going in. It says we've got a problem. And we'd better start dealing with it now.

I thought that Bush must have just gotten so caught up in his determination to convince the public that Social Security faces a crisis that he let down his guard, and the truth just slipped out. He knew better than anyone that every penny of the $509 billion in Social Security surplus generated during his first term was spent on government programs. He was fully aware that he was continuing to spend more than $400 million of Social Security surplus each and every day. However, since Bush's actions are a direct violation of his solemn pledge to the public that he would not touch any of the Social Security surplus, and since his misuse of Social Security funds is a violation of federal law, I did not expect the President to openly admit to his transgressions for the public record as he did on February 9.

I thought Bush's advisers were probably busily making plans for damage control if the remarks were widely reported in the media, and that Karl Rove and others were quietly hoping that nobody picked up on the importance of what the President said.   But when Bush made similar statements on Thursday in both North Carolina and Pennsylvania, it became obvious that the administration had decided to take a calculated risk and begin using the empty trust fund as part of the effort to convince the public that Social Security was in crisis.

On February 10, 2005, President Bush made the following statement about the trust fund during a speech in Pennsylvania.

"Now, one of the myths about Social Security is there's a pile of money sitting there accumulating, because you put money in, the government saves it for you, and then when you retire you get it out. That's not the way the system works. Every dime that goes in from payroll taxes is spent. It's spent on retirees, and if there's excess, it's spent on government programs. The only thing that Social Security has is a pile of IOUs from one part of government to the next."

This was a clear admission by the President of The United States that all Social Security surplus money had been spent and that President Bush was continuing to spend Social Security money each and every day. The president was verifying everything I had been saying for the past four years.

I felt sure the president's acknowledgment would make the Social Security trust fund fraud the leading news story the following day, but it was barely covered by the media. I thought the American people would now be able to see clearly that the only reason Bush was pushing for Social Security reform was that he knew there was no money in the trust fund. How could he not know? He has spent every dollar of the Social Security surplus since the day he took office, and he continues to spend all surplus Social Security revenue on a daily basis.

I thought Bush's admission that the trust fund has been raided and that it doesn't hold any real assets would be the beginning of the revelation of the great Social Security fraud that had been going on for more than two decades and involves both the Democrats and the Republicans. I knew that the American people were going to become very angry when they finally realized that they had been ripped off by their government. The question was how long it would take for journalists who had been intimidated by the Bush administration to overcome their fear of tackling politically explosive stories.

In hindsight, I am now beginning to wonder whether or not the Bush administration had all that much choice in the matter. Tidbits of the truth were already beginning to leak out, and the Bush advisers may have believed that it would be better for them to expose the empty trust fund than to have to defend why they were keeping it secret whenever it finally became breaking news.

On January 21, 2005, less than three weeks before the White House first acknowledged the empty trust fund, Comptroller General David Walker of the GAO made the following statement.

"The left hand owes the right hand, and that has legal, political and moral significance. But it doesn't have any economic significance whatsoever. There are no stocks or bonds or real estate in the trust fund. It has nothing of real value to draw down ... The trust fund gives a very false sense of security about where we are and how much time we have."

The Comptroller General of the GAO probably is the most credible source in the nation when it comes to telling the truth about governments actions. Instead of just saying that the trust fund holds no real assets, Walker specifically gave a list of things that the trust fund did not have. Most people already knew that the trust fund did not own stocks or real estate, but almost everyone was sure that it held Treasury bonds. When the Comptroller General specifically said that the trust fund does not hold any "bonds" he was sending a loud and clear message to those who thought otherwise.

Unfortunately, this statement was not widely reported. The San Francisco Chronicle was the only major newspaper I was able to find that carried it. (Carolyn Lochhead, San Francisco Chronicle, January 22, 2005)

In the February 14 issue of Newsweek, Allan Sloan wrote, "The money isn't being saved. Instead, one part of the government, the Treasury, is writing IOUs to another part, Social Security...The trust fund's irrelevant, folks. It's an accounting entry, not real money. How the Democrats can cling to the trust fund with a straight face is beyond me."

On Thursday, April 28, 2005, during a nationally televised news conference, President Bush said, *"Our system is called pay as you go. You pay into the system though your payroll taxes and the government spends it. It spends the money on the current retirees and with the money left over, it funds other programs. And all that's left behind is file cabinets full of IOUs."*

This is quite a contrast to what the President said on February 27, 2001 in his State of the Union address: *"To make sure the retirement savings of America's seniors are not diverted in any other program, my budget protects...the Social Security surplus for Social Security, and for Social Security alone."*

The current Social Security "crisis" is the direct result of the government's raiding and spending the surplus revenue generated by the 1983 payroll tax increase. The problem began with President George H. W. Bush who used Social Security money as if it were general fund revenue from day one of his presidency. The practice has continued ever since, so the $1.7 trillion in Social Security surplus revenue generated by the 1983 payroll tax increase, and earmarked specifically for funding the retirement of the baby boomers, is gone.

The baby boomers are not the cause of the Social Security problem. Alan Greenspan and company saw to it that the baby boomers would pay enough taxes to prepay the cost of their own retirement, in addition to funding the retirement of the generation that came before them. If the government had not raided the money, there would be enough assets in the trust fund to pay full benefits until at least 2041. And the 2041 actuarial imbalance could be corrected by removing the payroll tax earnings cap.

CHAPTER TWO

The Social Security Trust Fund

*Government is a trust, and the officers of govern-
ment are trustees; and both the trust and the
trustees are created for the benefit of the people.*

--Henry Clay

The United States was one of the last
advanced nation's in the world to establish a social
security system. In a speech to Congress on
January 17, 1935, President Franklin D. Roosevelt
urged passage of the Social Security Act. Roosevelt
said, "It is a sound idea—a sound ideal. Most of the
other advanced countries of the world have already
adopted it and their experience affords the
knowledge that social insurance can be made a
sound and workable project."

President Roosevelt stressed the importance
of developing a "self-sustaining" system whose
funds would be separate from general government
financing. He said, "The system adopted, except

for the money necessary to initiate it, should be self-sustaining in the sense that funds for the payment of insurance benefits should not come from the proceeds of general taxation."

With passage of the Social Security Act of 1935, America joined the rest of the advanced world in making a commitment to provide a financially sound social security system that would at least take some of the worry out of the financial consequences of growing old. Until recent decades, Americans have felt confident that their retirement benefits would be available when they needed them. They trusted their government to manage the funds wisely and responsibly. However, the events of the past two decades have led many Americans to question the commitment of current politicians to keeping the fund solvent for future generations.

The Social Security program has to some degree become a source of political maneuvering and a mask for irresponsible fiscal policies. Most of the abuse and misuse of the Social Security Trust Fund followed passage of legislation in 1983 which was supposed to raise—not lower—confidence in the long-term solvency of the program.

Fed Chairman, Alan Greenspan's warnings in February and August 2004 that future Social Security benefits would have to be cut were the opening scene of the well-orchestrated plot to raise public anxiety over Social Security's future. There is little doubt that Greenspan's announcements were coordinated with the secret Bush plan to attempt to dismantle the program. They set the stage for Bush to announce his privatization proposal at the convention.

But the stakes were too high, and the race was too close, for Bush to risk putting much emphasis on Social Security reform during the election campaign. Karl Rove had masterminded one plan to get Bush re-elected, and a separate plan to be implemented during Bush's second term once he had won the election. Moral issues would be the primary theme of the campaign. The campaign goals were to paint Bush as having higher moral values than his opponent, downplay the war in Iraq, and convince the voters that the massive Bush income tax cuts had put our economy on the road to long-term prosperity.

However, once Bush was safely elected to a second term, the plan to destroy Social Security would be put on the front burner. And that is what happened. Bush immediately began to use scare tactics in an attempt to convince the public that Social Security was in deep trouble, and that part of the solution would be partial privatization of the system.

A major part of the Bush campaign to destroy Social Security was to convince the public that the Social Security trust fund was really just a myth. He even traveled to Parkersburg, West Virginia to visit a Bureau of Public Debt office where the paper version of the $1.7 trillion in IOUs that represent the debt to the Social Security trust fund are stored in a file cabinet.

In a speech at West Virginia University at Parkersburg a short time after he viewed the file cabinet, Bush said, "Imagine. The retirement security for future generations is sitting in a filing cabinet. It's time to strengthen and modernize

Social Security for future generations with growing assets that you can control, that you call your own—assets that the government can't take away."

What Bush didn't say was that the only reason the Social Security trust fund is empty is because he, his father, and Bill Clinton have embezzled and spent every dime of the $1.7 trillion that is supposed to be in the trust fund. He didn't tell his audience that his administration had spent more than $400 million in Social Security surplus revenue that very day on other government programs. He did not tell the public that he financed his huge income tax cuts, that disproportionately benefited the rich, with the Social Security contributions of working Americans.

In 1983, legislation was enacted to improve the solvency of the Social Security Trust Fund which had run small budget deficits for seven years in a row from 1976-1982. The legislation, was in response to a recommendation the previous year by a Presidential Commission headed by Alan Greenspan. It was designed specifically for the purpose of building up a surplus in the Trust Fund in preparation for the staggering new obligations the fund would face when the baby-boom generation begins retiring about 2010. Both Social Security tax rates and the Social Security tax base were gradually raised over a seven-year period so the Trust Fund would be solvent when it took the big financial hit resulting from the retirement of the baby boomers, the largest generation in American history.

Unfortunately, instead of using the increased Social Security revenue to build up the size of the Trust Fund for future retirees as was intended, the government began using the surplus to fund other government programs as soon as it first appeared in 1983, and it has continued to do so ever since. This practice has masked the true size of federal budget deficits because each year since 1983 the government subtracted the surplus in the Social Security Trust Fund from the deficit in the operating budget and reported an official budget deficit that was billions of dollars below the actual deficit.

This issue came to a head in 1990 when Senator Daniel Patrick Moynihan of New York sent shock waves throughout Washington and much of the nation with his proposal to cut Social Security taxes. Senator Moynihan had been a strong supporter of the 1983 efforts to strengthen the Social Security system. He had served on the commission that recommended the plan that involved gradually raising the Social Security tax rate and raising the tax base.

Senator Moynihan was outraged that, instead of being used to build up the size of the Social Security Trust Fund for future retirees as was intended, the surplus was being used to pay for general government spending. Senator Moynihan, who felt the American people were being betrayed and deceived, proposed undoing the 1983 legislation by cutting Social Security taxes and returning the system to a "pay-as-you-go" basis which would have provided only enough revenue to take care of current retirees.

Moynihan took the position that if the government couldn't keep its hands out of the Social Security cookie jar, the jar should be emptied so there would be no Social Security surplus. He thought it was very dangerous and deceptive for the government to use the surplus in the Social Security Trust Fund to pay for general government spending, and thus proposed cutting Social Security taxes so there would be no surplus to mask the enormous deficits in the operating budget.

Cutting Social Security taxes wasn't really what Moynihan wanted. He had been a member of the Presidential Commission that had recommended the higher taxes, and he was a strong supporter of the legislation that enacted the higher taxes for purposes of strengthening the solvency of the Social Security Trust Fund. What Moynihan was really doing was blowing the whistle on the government for using the surplus for general government spending and then giving the impression that the deficit in the government's operating budget was tens of billions of dollars below what it actually was.

President George H.W. Bush, who had said over and over on the campaign trail, "Read my lips. No new taxes," opposed Senator Moynihan's plan to cut Social Security taxes. If the government had not had the Social Security surplus from which to borrow, it would have been forced to either raise taxes or report much larger budget deficits to the public. In response to reporters' questions about Senator Moynihan's proposal to cut Social Security taxes, Bush replied, "It is an effort to get me to raise taxes on the American people by the charade of cutting them, or cut benefits, and I am not going to do it to the older people of this country."

But President Bush was in fact taking money from a fund that was supposed to be used to provide for "the older people of this country" and using it to fund general government. During George H.W. Bush's four years as President, the Social Security Trust Fund ran surpluses totaling $211.7 billion. Every dollar of that Social Security surplus was borrowed and used by the Bush administration to fund other government programs. Since not a penny of that debt was repaid during the Bush Senior Presidency, higher taxes will have to be levied against the American people at some point in the future partly to repay the money that the "Read-my-lips-no-new-taxes" president borrowed from the Social Security Fund.

President George H.W. Bush followed a practice that began during the second Reagan term and has continued ever since. That practice is to spend the dollars generated by Social Security taxes just like any other taxes, even though Social Security funds are required by law to be kept separate from other funds.

One of the reasons that it has been so easy for the government to deceive the American people about the true financial condition of the United States Government is the fact that any Social Security surplus funds are by law supposed to be invested in financial instruments "backed by the full faith and credit of the United States government." Under current law, the Social Security funds cannot be invested in stocks, commercial bonds, real estate, or even FDIC insured bank accounts. They must be invested in government securities.

However, this does not in any way necessitate or justify the using of surplus funds to finance general government operations. Every dollar of Social Security revenue in excess of what is required to pay current benefits should be used to pay down the gigantic national debt by investing the surplus in public issue marketable Treasury bonds, purchased in the open market from private investors. Doing so would have the equivalent effect of putting the money into a separate bank account that was off limits to politicians who were tempted to borrow the funds to pay for general government operations.

Instead of saving the surplus and investing it in marketable Treasury bonds, the government has been spending all of the Social Security surplus and issuing a special type of non-marketable government IOU called special issue Treasury securities which are not real bonds. These special issues are available to and held by only the government trust funds.

Unlike the marketable Treasury bonds that are "good-as-gold," and can be sold in the open market at any time, the special issue IOUs cannot be sold to anyone even for a penny on the dollar. They are simply a promise that the government will repay the "borrowed" Social Security money at some time in the future. However, the government has been spending the money and issuing the IOUs since 1983, and absolutely no provisions have been made for repaying any of the looted Social Security money.

Using Social Security surplus funds to pay down the national debt during the Social Security surplus years between 1984 and 2017, and then borrowing the money back to supplement the inadequate payroll tax revenue in the years after 2017 when Social Security will be running deficits, would have been the fiscally responsible thing to do. The surplus money would have been invested in government securities as required by law, but it would not have been available for funding general government programs.

Unfortunately, President George H.W. Bush chose instead to use the Social Security surplus as a giant slush fund.   He diverted the entire $211.7 billion of surplus payroll tax revenue that flowed in during his presidency to the general fund for spending on other government programs.

Although President Clinton did reduce the huge budget deficits, he also participated in the charade that portrayed government finances as being much better than they actually were. Clinton also used the Social Security surpluses for general government financing.

The Budget Enforcement Act of 1990 made substantial changes in the budget process. Among these changes was the removal of the income and outgo of the Social Security Trust Funds from all calculations of the Federal budget, including the budget deficit or surplus. This exclusion applied to the budget prepared by the President, the Federal budgets formulated by the Congress, and to the budget process provisions designed to reduce and control the budget deficits. (Section 13301, the

"Hollings amendment" prohibited including Social Security in any budget calculation)

The Social Security Trust Fund was always supposed to be kept separate from the government's operating budget. However, in 1969, a time when Congress did not have a budget-making process, President Lyndon Johnson administratively began officially counting Social Security funds as part of the Federal Budget. In 1974, with passage of the Congressional Budget and Impoundment Control Act, Congress adopted a process for developing budget goals and, these also officially counted Social Security as part of the "unified budget."

These actions did not set well with the public, and Senator Moynihan's efforts to make the public aware of just how the Social Security money was being used led to concerns that the public's confidence in the program was being eroded. The increased public awareness also led to proposals to legally remove Social Security from the budget. Finally, in 1990, Congress reacted to the criticism that surplus Social Security taxes were masking the size of the budget deficits by legally removing Social Security from the budget calculations. (Section 13301 of The Budget Enforcement Act of 1990.)

CHAPTER THREE

From the 1983 "Fix" to the 2005 "Crisis"

"..The most reprehensible fraud in this great jambalaya of frauds is the systematic and total ransacking of the Social security trust fund...The Treasury is siphoning off every dollar of the Social Security surplus to meet current operating expenses of the Government...The American people will wake up to the reality that those IOUs in the trust fund vault are a 21st century version of Confederate banknotes."

--Senator Ernest (Fritz) Hollings, Speech on Senate Floor October 13, 1989

The Social Security Amendments of 1983 provided for raising payroll taxes high enough so that there would be an annual surplus for the next three decades. The surplus revenue was supposed to be saved and invested in order to build up a large reserve in the trust fund with which to help pay for the retirement of the baby boomers. Prior to the

1983 tax hike there had been no significant surplus in the Social Security fund, so the government had never had the opportunity to misuse Social Security money before. In fact, the trust fund had run small budget deficits for seven consecutive years from 1976 through 1982.

That all changed with enactment of the surplus-generating tax hike of 1983. The annual surplus grew from $9.4 billion in 1985 to $33.8 billion in 1988. By 1998, it was $99.2 billion, and Social Security revenue will exceed Social Security benefit payments by approximately $160 billion in 2005. Social Security will continue to run annual surpluses until 2017 when the decades of surpluses will end and accelerating annual deficits will begin as a result of the retirement of the baby boomers. The tax increase generated $1.7 trillion in surplus Social Security revenue between 1984 and 2005, and an additional $2.0 trillion will be generated between 2005 and 2017.

If the Social Security surplus revenue had been saved and invested, as was the intent of the 1983 law, the trust fund would hold $3.7 trillion in real assets by 2017 when the surpluses will come to an end. That would be enough assets to assure payment of full Social Security benefits until at least 2041 when the youngest of the baby boomers would be 77 years old.

The 1983 Social Security fix almost did the job, but it was a little off the mark. Beginning in 2041, the payroll tax revenue will only be sufficient to pay approximately 74 percent of promised benefits. Therefore, there is a small actuarial imbalance that needs to be corrected. This is only a minor problem that could be solved in a number of ways. One way to solve that problem would be to remove the cap on earnings subject to Social Security payroll taxes. That cap is currently $90,000. This means that all earnings above $90,000 are tax-exempt. If the cap were removed, and everybody paid payroll taxes on all their earnings just as they do in the case of the income tax, this would be sufficient revenue to correct the actuarial imbalance, and the Social Security fund would be solvent for at least 75 more years in the accounting sense.

I qualified the above statement by saying the trust fund would be solvent "in the accounting sense." This means that if all the Social Security surplus revenue had been saved and invested as it was supposed to be, and the earnings cap was removed, we would not have a Social Security problem for at least another 75 years. Unfortunately, the Social Security surplus revenue has not been saved and invested. Every dollar of the $1.7 trillion in Social Security surplus generated so far has been "borrowed" by the government and spent on other things.

Actually "borrowed" is not the appropriate word to describe what has happened to the Social Security contributions of working Americans. The word, borrowed, implies repayment, but absolutely no provisions have been made for the repayment of any of the money spent over the past 21 years. If the money is never repaid to the Social Security trust fund, as some are suggesting, then the money has been stolen. Every penny of the $1.7 trillion dollars in surplus Social Security revenue has been embezzled by the government over the past 21 years, and the government is continuing to embezzle more than $400 million in additional Social Security surplus money each and every day.

Words such as, "embezzlement", "thievery", "stealing", and "fraud" were being used by United States Senators in speeches on the Senate floor fifteen years ago to describe what was happening to the Social Security money in an effort to get President George H.W. Bush to stop raiding the trust fund.   Senator Patrick Daniel Moynihan of New York even introduced legislation in 1990 to roll back the 1983 payroll tax increase in an effort to keep Bush from spending it.   There was substantial news coverage of the issue at that time. The article below is an op-ed piece that I wrote for the Denver Post in 1990.

THE DENVER POST

Monday, March 5, 1990

VIEWPOINT: Has the Social Security Trust Fund Been Mismanaged?

Current practices both deceptive and dangerous

By Allen W. Smith

Sen. Daniel Patrick Moynihan of New York sent political and economic shock waves throughout Washington and much of the nation with his proposal to cut Social Security taxes. Although his proposal has received support from the conservative Heritage Foundation, the liberal Institute of Policy Studies and the U.S. Chamber of Commerce, it is strongly opposed by the Bush administration.

"It is an effort to get me to raise taxes on the American people by the charade of cutting them, or cut benefits," Bush told reporters. "And I am not going to do it to the older people of this country."

The controversy goes much deeper than the question of whether to cut Social Security taxes. It involves alleged mismanagement of the Social Security Trust Fund and charges that deceptive accounting practices are understating the size of the Federal Budget Deficit by more than $50 billion per year.

The controversy dates back to 1983 when measures were adopted to build up the Social Security Trust Fund in order to meet soaring benefit costs that will occur when the baby boom generation begins reaching retirement age 20 years from now.

Senator Moynihan was a strong supporter of the 1983 efforts to strengthen the Social Security system. He served on the commission that recommended the plan that involved gradually raising the Social Security tax rate from 6.7 percent in 1983 to 7.65 percent in 1990, and raising the tax base from $35,700 in 1983 to $51,300 in 1990. The latest increase, which went into effect Jan. 1, raised Social Security taxes by $320 a year for people earning $51,300 or more.

The problem is that, instead of being used to build up the size of the Social Security Trust Fund for future retirees as was intended, the surplus in the Social Security fund is being used to pay for general government spending by investing it in Treasury securities.

This practice masks the true size of the federal budget deficit. The projected federal budget deficit for this year is being reported as $141 billion. This official measure of the deficit is $65 billion below the real projected deficit of $206 billion. The government is deducting an expected $65 billion surplus in the Social Security Trust Fund from the real expected deficit (the difference between total federal spending and revenue from all sources except Social Security).

The real deficit for fiscal 1989 was also above $200 billion, but was reported as much less because of last year's $55 billion surplus in the Social Security fund.

The current surpluses in the Trust Fund were supposed to be set aside to build up the fund which will face staggering obligations when the baby boom generation begins retiring about 2010.

Instead, the surplus Social Security money is being used to finance current government spending programs. Outraged by this practice, Senator Moynihan proposes cutting Social Security taxes and returning the system to a "pay-as-you-go" basis which will provide only enough revenue to take care of current retirees.

If the government can't keep its hand out of the Social Security cookie jar, Senator Moynihan wants the cookie jar emptied so there is no Social Security surplus.

Current government practices are dangerous on two counts. First, by masking the size of the federal budget deficit, the government is misleading the American people and giving the impression that the deficit problem is less serious than it actually is.

Contrary to popular belief, the federal budget deficit has not been steadily declining in recent years. The on-budget deficit (the difference between total federal spending and total revenue, excluding Social Security contributions) was $169.3 billion in fiscal 1987, $193.9 billion in fiscal 1988, and more than $200 billion in fiscal 1989. The idea that the budget deficit problem is improving is a cruel hoax.

The second major misconception is that the Social Security system, that was supposedly repaired seven years ago, is currently actuarially sound for the long term.

At the moment, the Social Security surplus exists only on paper. The actual funds have been used to help finance the day-to-day operations of the federal government . The funds have been replaced with Treasury certificates that offer only a pledge that the government will fulfill its obligations to future retirees by somehow raising the money in the future.

Current practices are both deceptive and dangerous.

Copyright 1990 Allen W. Smith

President George Bush was infuriated by Moynihan's proposal to roll back the payroll tax increase so there would no longer be surplus Social Security revenue. Bush, the "read-my-lips-no-new-taxes" president was using every dollar of the Social

Security surplus to help fund his huge budget deficits. If he were deprived of the Social Security surplus revenue for his slush fund, he might have to call for higher income taxes.

On January 24, 1990, President George H. W. Bush held a news conference in which he was put on the defensive for his use of Social Security taxes to fund general government operating expenses. The president was asked a number of pointed questions that gave him ample opportunity to deny, or try to justify, the use of these surpluses. But Bush evaded every single question, in essence leaving the impression that all the harsh criticism was valid. The following are excerpts from the president's news conference.

Q. Mr. President, over the last few years there have been large increases in the Social Security tax. And even though it's a regressive tax, people supported it, or swallowed it, because they were told that that was necessary to make the system solvent for the next generation. But now everyone is finding out that, in fact, that money isn't there any longer, that it's been used for debt reduction. Given the fact that people are now realizing that this is happening, do you think it's fair to ask them to continue to pay this increased tax for even 1 month longer?

A. *The Commission that reformed Social Security was well-aware of what you've just talked about. They considered it.   I think the Commission included Mr. Moynihan—I may be mistaken, but I think it did.   And they considered this point.   And we will have some innovative suggestions as we go along here as to how to compensate for this understandable concern on the part of some. But for now, for this year, we will not alter the recommendations of that bipartisan commission.*

Q. Could I just briefly—do you feel that this increase was sold to people under false premises?

A. *No, because I think these were intelligent people wrestling with a very, very difficult problem, and I can't accuse them of selling the Commission conclusion as under false cover.*

Q. Well, as you know, the budget deficit has been coming down over the past few years solely because the Social Security surplus has been rising. In fact, your own budget projections show $200 billion a year deficits in the indefinite future when you remove the Social Security surplus. Given the fact that you have such a large deficit in every other program, when will you and the Congress stop both bickering and accountant gimmicks and deal with this problems that the American public has said for a decade---

A. *Thank you for the endorsement of our approach, Owen . We would urge that we stop bickering and go forward with the proposal that we come out with, that I think will begin to address itself to*

Maureen's question, that is very sound. And nobody's trying to conceal the fact that the Social Security Trust Fund is operating at a surplus. ...

Q. Well, wait. If I could follow, sir: Your own budget proposal that you will unveil on Monday, which shows a $64 billion deficit, in fact, if you remove Social Security, would be closer to $150 billion. Is that not correct?

A. *But you're making the old argument of taking the Social Security Trust Fund off budget. And at this juncture we're not prepared to do that. But wait until you see the detail, and I hope the American people will see something here that begins to address itself to these fundamentals that I think are properly being asked about.*

Reporters turned to other subject categories at this point, but near the end of the news conference Social Security taxes came up once again.

Q. Mr. President, another question that's been raised about the Moynihan proposal is the fairness of the tax system. Over the past decade, even as income tax has come down for high-paid people, Social Security taxes have gone up, mostly for lower and middle-income people. Do you think that's fair?

A.   *Well, look, if we were all starting over, I think we could fine-tune the entire tax system.   We're not starting over.   And I think that system has been in and out over the years, basically a pretty fair system. ....*

Q. But, sir, some of your favorite economists in think tanks say that the Social Security tax acts as a great disincentive to work and to employing people.

A. *Yes*

Q. Doesn't that serve the same end?

A.   *Well, I think that's a legitimate complaint about some of it, and that's one of the reasons I favor holding the line on taxes.   And one of the reasons I oppose Moynihan is I think it's a disguise for increased taxes around the corner.   And I don't want to see the benefits of Social Security cut.   It is odd that a Republican President, often accused by political opponents in an election year, is the one that is protecting the sanctity of the Social Security benefits.   And I would say to those out around the country: Take a hard look now—don't let that rabbit be pulled out of the hat by 1 hand and 25 other rabbits dumped on you in another.   This is a very complicated situation, and this is a sleight of hand operation here. ...*

The president had ample opportunity during that news conference to explain why he was using Social Security money for other government programs and to mask the true size of the budget deficits. He also had the opportunity to deny the fact that he was indeed engaged in such fraudulent behavior, and the opportunity to offer some explanation that might justify what he was doing. But the president neither denied the accusation nor gave any justification for misappropriation of the Social Security money.

In essence, President Bush admitted to the misuse of Social Security funds by totally evading the questions. He also demonstrates almost a total lack of knowledge of the Social Security Commission. If he wasn't even sure whether or not Senator Moynihan, one of the most vocal members, was on the Commission, how could he possibly have known the in-depth recommendations of the Commission?

Senator Moynihan responded to the President's accusation that he was engaged in a sleight of hand operation on the Senate floor later that day.

Mr. MOYNIHAN.   I thank my distinguished, gallant, generous colleague from New Jersey for giving me this opportunity.

Mr. President.
I rise for a painful purpose—to state my disappointment in the remarks made by the President this morning at his press conference in response to questions concerning my legislation to return the Social Security System to pay-as-you-go financing. I introduced the bill yesterday in the company of a number of colleagues, having said on December 29 that I would do so.

Mr. President, there is no "sleight of hand" involved whatever. I do not see that there was any need to make such a characterization. If there is a problem of dissimulation, I would suggest it resides with the present practice of using Social Security trust funds as general revenues. My distinguished friend, the Republican Senator from Pennsylvania, Senator Heinz, has used a very direct word for this. He says it is called "embezzlement."

Moynihan was the target of much criticism from Republicans for daring to force the government into being honest about its finances. On April 4, 1990, Tom Ridge, then a Congressman from Pennsylvania requested permission to address the house with regard to the Moynihan proposal.

Mr. Ridge. Mr. Speaker, I rise today to express my opposition to Senator Moynihan's plan to cut the Social Security payroll tax and to express my surprise that the Democratic National Committee endorses it.

Mr. Speaker, this proposal endangers the Social Security trust fund reserves and could lead to substantially higher taxes when current obligations become due. The Moynihan proposal puts the future stability and integrity of the Social Security system in doubt and only creates problems where solutions are needed. It is unfair to future generations to eliminate reserves created for them and paid for by them.

Mr. Speaker, I do not know why the Democrats would endorse such a plan eagerly. Maybe they simply saw a surplus that they could not figure out a way to spend.

We may not know why the Democrats may want to threaten Social Security, but the American people should know that President Bush and the Republicans will try to do all they can to keep those Democratic hands off those Social Security benefits.

This was the ultimate in political spin and character assassination. From its very beginning, the Social Security system was opposed by many Republicans, and counting on Republicans to protect Social Security would be like placing a fox in the chicken house to guard the chickens. Social Security was always the Democrat's baby, and some Democrats spent their entire political careers trying to protect it. Senator Moynihan was one such person. He was without doubt one of the greatest friends that Social Security had ever had. Moynihan had served on the 1982 Commission to reform Social Security, and he served on President George W. Bush's Social Security Commission. For Ridge, who was participating in President Bush's Social Security fraud to deceive the American public, to claim that President Bush and the Republicans were trying to save the Social Security reserves, every dollar of which had already been embezzled, was outrageous.

George Herbert Walker Bush was the president who set the precedent for using Social Security dollars to fund other government programs. The Social Security trust fund ran surpluses totaling $211.7 billion during Bush's four-year term, and Bush spent every dollar of the surplus funds on other government programs. He ran average annual on-budget deficits of more than $286 billion per year, and the national debt, that had been only $1 trillion at the beginning of the Reagan-Bush administration, had soared above the $4 trillion mark by the time Bush left office.

President George Bush followed one of the most irresponsible fiscal polices in the nation's history, and his actions speak loud and clear. However, in his effort to deceive the American people, Bush wore a mask of innocence and good intentions. He tried to persuade the public that he cared deeply about the nation's financial future at the same time that he was fraudulently undermining it through accounting trickery and other shenanigans.

On the evening of October 2, 1990, President George Bush went on national television in an attempt to persuade the public to pressure their representatives in Congress to vote for a proposed budget that Senator Hollings described as "the worst budget document I have ever seen." Excerpts from the President's speech are reproduced below.

"Tonight, I want to talk to you about a problem that has lingered and dogged and vexed this country for far too long: the federal budget deficit. Thomas Paine said many years ago, "These are the times that try men's souls." As we speak, our nation is standing together against Saddam Hussein's aggression. But here at home, there is another threat, a cancer gnawing away at our nation's health. That cancer is the budget deficit. Year after year, it mortgages the future of our children.

No family, no nation, can continue to do business the way the federal government has been operating and survive. When you get a bill, that bill must be paid, and when you write a check, you're supposed to have money in the bank. But if you don't obey these simple rules of common sense, there is a price to pay. But for too long, the nation's business in Washington has been conducted as if these basic rules did not apply. Well, these rules do apply. And if we fail to act, next year alone we will face a federal budget deficit of more than $300 billion, a deficit that *could weaken our economy further and cost us thousands of precious jobs. ...*

...This is the first time in my presidency that I have made an appeal like this to you, the American people. With your help we can at last put this budget crisis behind us and face the other challenges that lie ahead. If we do, the long-term result will be a healthier nation and something more. We will have once again put ourselves on the path of economic growth and we will have demonstrated that no challenge is greater than the determination of the American people.

Thank you, God bless you and good night."

The speech was a superb reminder of the basic rules that apply to sound fiscal management for individuals, businesses, and the government. It is hard to imagine any American not agreeing with the words in this speech. It sure sounded like the president was concerned about the nation's financial future, and he appeared to be against mortgaging our children's future. If he was being sincere and honest with the American people, how could we fail to support policies with such noble goals?

That's the catch. Just like a gifted con-artist, the president was saying one thing and doing something very different. He was trying to convince the public that his policies would lead to an outcome that would be for the common good—one that almost everyone could agree on—when, in reality, they did just the opposite. He and his advisers must have been amused at how easy it was for him to pull the wool over the eyes of the American public.

The following day, Senator Hollings rose on the Senate floor and requested that the President's speech be printed in full in the Congressional Record. There being no objection, the material was ordered to be printed in the Record.

Then Senator Hollings gave his assessment of the proposed budget bill.

...It is supposed to solve the deficit problem. Instead it adds $1.2 trillion to the national debt over the 5-year period. That is using the figures given to us by Director Richard Darman of the Office of Management and Budget. Indeed this agreement expressly abandons any pretense of trying to eliminate the deficits. Instead, it talks about "proposed savings."...There is no serious deficit reduction purpose. There is a serious purpose of deceit and fraud upon the American people. ....

...I can tell you here and now this is the worst budget document I have ever seen gliding through this body. ...I fought on this floor against Kemp-Roth, Reaganomics, which George Herbert Walker Bush called voodoo economics. Now he is a high priest of voodoo, a national distributor of voodoo last night on TV, I can tell you that.

This wasn't the first time that Senator Hollings had lambasted the Bush policy of raiding the Social Security trust fund and using the proceeds as if it were general revenue. Nearly a year earlier, on October 13, 1989, Senator Hollings expressed his outrage at the fraudulent practices that had been taking place. The entire text of the speech is reproduced below from the Congressional Record {Page: S13411}

Mr. HOLLINGS. Mr. President, this morning I joined with the distinguished majority leader, Senator Mitchel, and others to unveil our proposal for taking the Social Security surpluses off budget for purposes of calculating compliance with Gramm-Rudman-Hollings.   This leadership initiative will be a critical first step toward restoring truth in Federal budgeting. And, let's face it, until we acknowledge the truth—the scale and enormity— of our deficits, then we will continue on our current wreckless course of do-nothingism, denial and deception.

The late John Mitchell, when he was Attorney General in the Nixon administration, used to say over and over again, "Watch what we do, not what we say." Well, the American people would do well to take that same advice if they want to understand just how desperate our current fiscal crisis really is.

Look not at what we are saying, but at what we are doing. We say that the budget deficit for 1990 will be just under $100 billion. Yet, lo and behold, at the end of this month we are going to raise the debt limit by some 300 billion dollars to allow for expected public borrowing during the fiscal year 1990. Now, if the deficit is only $100 billion, why are we going to borrow $300 billion? The answer is simple. We are going to borrow $300 billion in 1990 because the true deficit, once you cut through all the monkeyshine, is going to be $300 billion. We arrive at that fanciful $100 billion projection only by indulging in enough fraud and larceny and malfeasance to land an ordinary citizen in the penitentiary.

Of course, the most reprehensible fraud in this great jambalaya of frauds is the systematic and total ransacking *of the Social Security trust fund in order to mask the true size of the deficit. As we all know, the Social Security payroll tax has become a money machine for the U.S. Treasury, generating fantastic revenue surpluses in excess of the costs of the Social Security program. Excess Social Security tax revenues will be $65 billion in 1990 alone— boosted by yet another rise in the Social Security tax rate, slated to kick in January 1. By 1993, the annual Social Security surplus will soar to $99 billion.*

The public fully supported enactment of hefty new Social Security taxes in 1983 to ensure the retirement program's long-term solvency and credibility. The promise was that today's huge surpluses would be set safely aside in a trust fund to provide for baby-boomer retirees in the next century.

Well, look again. The Treasury is siphoning off every dollar of the Social Security surplus to meet current operating expenses of the Government. By thus reducing the deficit, we mask the true enormity of the Federal budget crisis while creating the illusion that Congress and the administration are actually doing something about deficits.

Mr. President, our proposed amendment, which we intend to attach to the debt-ceiling bill, would put Social Security surpluses off budget for purposes of calculating the Federal budget deficit beginning October 1, the first day of fiscal 1990. The distinguished junior Senator from Texas and his Republican colleagues, aiming to rescue the administration's read my lips strategy, plan an alternative amendment that would put Social Security off budget in the distant future, in 1994.

By 1994, however, a cumulative sum, in excess of a half-trillion dollars, will have been borrowed from the Social Security trust fund, and the denuded trust fund will be piled high with IOU's. Those IOU's are a charming bookkeeping nicety, but the sheriff who tries to collect on them is truly going to have his work cut out for him.

The hard fact is that, in the next century, the Social Security system will find itself paying out vastly more in benefits than it is taking in through payroll taxes. And the American people will wake up to the reality that those IOU's in the trust fund vault are a 21st century version of Confederate banknotes.

Of course, the Treasury would have the option of raising taxes to repay the astronomical sums we have borrowed from the trust fund. But that would be a brazen ripoff of working Americans, many of whom will be retirees obliged to pay a second time for the benefits they have already earned.

On the other hand, if the Treasury wimps out and chooses not to raise taxes to reimburse the trust fund, then there will be no alternative but to slash Social Security benefits. The most likely scenario is that Social Security payments would be turned into just another means-tested welfare program for the very poor; if you make more than say, $15,000 per year, then forget about collecting any Social Security benefits.

Any way you slice it, it is a lousy public policy to borrow massively from the Social Security trust fund with no credible plan for reimbursement. Of course, the immediate damage from this approach is that it allows us to mask the true scale of the Federal budget deficit, thus making it easier for us politicians to sit on our hands.

This is a gross breach of faith with the American people. Social Security is perhaps the most successful social program ever enacted by the Federal Government. Without question, it is the most effective antipoverty program in history. Social Security is not charity or welfare. On the contrary, it is a supplementary retirement fund that workers pay for with their hard-earned money.

I say it is time to stop playing games with Social Security and the government's finances. It is time to use honest budget numbers and to make honest budget choices. By all means, let us begin by putting Social Security truly in trust and totally off budget.

Mr. President, I ask unanimous consent that the text of my original bill be printed in the Record at this point.

Senator Hollings' proposal eventually became Section 13301 of the Budget Enforcement Act of 1990, which was signed into law by President Bush on November 5, 1990. It prohibited including Social Security funds in any budget calculations including deficits or surpluses.

Section 13301 explicitly states:
Not withstanding any other provision of law, the receipts and disbursements of the Federal Old Age and Survivors Insurance Trust Fund and the Federal Disability Insurance Trust Fund shall not be counted as new budget authority, outlays, receipts, or deficit or surplus for purposes of   (1) the budget of the United States

Government as submitted by the President, (2) the Congressional budget, or (3) the Balanced Budget and Emergency Deficit Control Act of 1985.

Senator Hollings thought that by making it illegal for the Congress and the President to include Social Security funds in their budget calculations the deliberate deception of the public would come to an end. But he was wrong. The Bush administration and many members of Congress got over this tiny hurdle by simply ignoring the law. They continued their deceptive practices just as they had done before. But there was a difference. Now they were guilty of more than deception. Now they were guilty of deliberately violating federal law.

President Clinton reversed the trend of larger and larger budget deficits. At the beginning of his first term, he pushed through Congress a deficit-reduction package, which included both tax increases and spending cuts. Republicans opposed this deficit-reduction package adamantly because it included higher taxes, and not a single Republican voted for the measure. The bill passed the Senate only by the tie-breaking vote of Vice President Al Gore, and Republicans insisted that the Clinton policy would wreck the economy.

Now, with the benefit of hindsight, we know that the deficits grew smaller and smaller, and the economy grew stronger and stronger throughout the Clinton Presidency. Finally, in 1999, the government experienced the first balanced budget in 40 years. Actually, a tiny surplus of $1.9 billion was reported after several revisions, but it was essentially a balanced budget. In Fiscal 2000, there was a non-Social Security surplus of $86.6 billion at a time that the economy was at the peak of the business cycle with the unemployment rate at a 30-year low.

The tiny surplus of 1999, and the more significant surplus in 2000, were the only true surpluses in the past 40 years. All the talk about surpluses as far as the eye could see was based on phony and fraudulent projections using unrealistic assumptions.

In fiscal 2001 the budget returned to deficit territory with a non-Social Security deficit of $32.5 billion, and in 2002, the deficit soared to $317.5 billion. We face massive deficits in the years ahead. In about 12 years, the Social Security fund will begin running deficits, in addition to the deficits in the general operating budget. Without radical changes in government policies, the fiscal future of the United States Government looks so bleak that nobody can be sure what kinds of catastrophes are ahead.

It's time to eradicate fraud from the federal government, and make public officials pay the same price for fraud that we are now demanding of corporate "wrongdoers." George W. Bush demanded that the CEOs of all private companies in America follow sound accounting practices and abide by the law. As the CEO of the largest firm in the world, Bush needs to practice what he preaches!

CHAPTER FOUR

The 2000 Campaign and The New Covenant

"Social Security is the single most successful program in government history...For years, politicians have dipped into the trust fund to pay for more spending. And I will stop it."

--George W. Bush, Speech in Rancho Cucamonga, California on May 15, 2000.

Al Gore made the raiding of the Social Security Trust Fund a major campaign issue in the 2000 election campaign. He promised that if he were elected President, all surplus Social Security revenue would be put in a lockbox for Social Security and Social Security alone. He pledged that Social Security surplus revenue would be used to pay Social Security benefits, and not a dollar of it would be spent on other government programs.

Not to be outdone, Republican candidate, George W. Bush, also pledged to end the raiding of the Social Security Trust Fund.

In a Florida speech on October 26, 2000, Bush said, "I'm going to set aside $2.4 trillion of Social Security surplus. That's $2.4 trillion more in payroll taxes than we owe the seniors, which means there is a really interesting opportunity to make sure we not only fulfill the promises to the seniors but we have a social security system that is hopeful for younger workers."

There could have been no doubt about George W. Bush's stand on the Social Security Trust Fund during the 2000 presidential campaign. He repeatedly promised that if he were elected President, he would end the practice of raiding the trust fund, and that Social Security revenue would only be spent on Social Security benefits. If anyone had any doubt about Bush's position, all they had to do was login to the Bush-Cheney 2000 website. There, in black and white, under the list of Position Proposals, was the emphatic statement, "The Social Security surplus must be locked away only for Social Security."

Despite the past raiding of the Social Security Trust Fund, those who voted for either Bush or Gore knew they were voting for a candidate who had entered into a new covenant with the American people promising to protect the trust fund from any future raiding. In short, the American people had every right to believe that the days of spending Social Security money on other government programs were over, no matter which candidate won the election.

Given the extremely close nature of the 2000 election, I think it is a safe bet to assume that neither candidate could have been elected if the public had known in advance that the promise would not be kept.   I further believe that the American people had a right to demand that whoever was elected would honor their pledge to protect the Social Security surplus.

Bush did not change his tune when he first became President.   He continued to insist that Social Security revenue would be used for Social Security and Social Security alone.   In his radio address to the nation on February 3, 2001, Bush said, *"My plan will keep all Social Security money in the Social Security system where it belongs."*

In his State of the Union Address on February 27, 2001, Bush was even more emphatic about his determination to keep his Social Security pledge.   He said, *To make sure the retirement savings of America's seniors are not diverted in any other program, my budget protects all $2.6 trillion of the Social Security surplus for Social Security, and for Social Security alone."*

Four days later, on March 3, 2001, Bush sought to eliminate any remaining doubt that might still exist about his sincere commitment to keep his hands out of the Social Security cookie jar with the following statement.

"We're going to keep the promise of Social Security and keep the government from raiding the Social Security surplus."

The previous raiding of the trust fund by Presidents George H. W. Bush and Bill Clinton is despicable.   However, at that time, the issue had never been subjected to a public debate where the American people could speak out on it.   That all changed as a result of the 2000 campaign and election. Every American voter who cast a vote for either Bush or Gore had a right to expect that the era of raiding the Social Security trust fund was over. They had entered into a new covenant with the future President of the United States in which it was mutually agreed that all future surplus Social Security revenue would be untouchable for any purpose other than the payment of Social Security benefits.

That covenant between President Bush and the American people is still in force. The President did not renegotiate the deal with the American people. He didn't even admit that he had reneged on the agreement during the 2004 campaign. I tried to alert the public throughout Bush's first term that he was spending the Social Security surplus, in violation of his promise to the American people, and in violation of federal law, but nobody would believe me.

In Bush's first State of the Union address, delivered on February 27, 2001, he laid the foundation for his plan to enact massive tax cuts that would benefit primarily the wealthiest 5 percent of Americans. He also skillfully pulled the wool over the eyes of the public through a series of deceptive statements designed to convince Congress that the coffers of the United States government were overflowing with billions of surplus dollars for as far as the eye could see. "Deceptive statements" is putting it mildly. To put it more bluntly, he lied to the American people about the financial status of the federal budget.

The following are excerpts from the speech.

"Our new governing vision says government should be active, but limited; engaged, but not overbearing. And my budget is based on that philosophy. It is reasonable, and it is responsible....My plan pays down an unprecedented amount of our national debt. And then, when money is still left over, my plan returns it to the people who earned it in the first place.

...To make sure the retirement savings of America's seniors are not diverted in any other program, my budget protects all $2.6 trillion of the Social Security surplus for Social Security, and for Social Security alone.

...My budget has funded a responsible increase in our ongoing operations. It has funded our nation's important priorities; it has protected Social Security and Medicare. And our surpluses are big enough that there is still money left over.

Many of you have talked about the need to pay down our national debt. I listened and I agree. We owe it to our children and grandchildren to act now, and I hope you will join me to pay down $2 trillion in debt during the next 10 years...That is more debt, repaid more quickly than has ever been repaid by any nation at any time in history.

We should also prepare for the unexpected, for the uncertainties of the future. We should approach our nation's budget as any prudent family would, with a contingency fund for emergencies or additional spending needs. For example, after a strategic review, we may need to increase defense spending. We may need to increase spending for our farmers or additional money to reform

Medicare. And so, my budget sets aside almost a trillion dollars over 10 years for additional needs. That is one trillion additional reasons you can feel comfortable supporting this budget.

We have increased our budget at a responsible 4 percent. We have funded our priorities. We paid down all the available debt. We have prepared for contingencies. And we still have money left over.

...Now we come to a fork in the road; we have two choices. ...We could spend the money on more and bigger government. That's the road our nation has traveled in recent years.

...If you continue on that road, you will spend the surplus and have to dip into Social Security to pay other bills. Unrestrained government spending is a dangerous road to deficits, so we must take a different path. The other choice is to let the American people spend their own money to meet their own needs.

I hope you will join me in standing firmly on the side of the people. You see, the growing surplus exists because taxes are too high and government is charging more that it needs. The people of America have been overcharged and, on their behalf, I am here asking for a refund."

Perhaps never before in history had the American people been played for such fools by their president. Most people know very little about such things as economics and the federal budget, so they must trust someone to tell them the truth. Surely they could trust a new president who was asking for their support to be straightforward with them. If he said the government had trillions of dollars of surplus money, it must be true, regardless of how implausible it seemed. And he wasn't the only top official to say so. Both President Clinton and Vice President Gore had spoken of large surpluses.

But, of course, there was the disturbing fact that many economists were saying that there was no surplus. On September 27, 2000, just exactly five months prior to the President's address, I appeared on CNN TODAY with Lou Waters to discuss my newly published book, *The Alleged Budget Surplus, Social Security, and Voodoo Economics.* Its basic theme was that there was no true surplus. I argued that the government had been lying to the American people for several years about the real status of the federal budget and the Social Security Trust Fund. I pointed out that there was not a single dollar of reserves in the Social Security Trust Fund because the government had been borrowing from the fund for several years and using the money to fund other programs.

Excerpts follow from the transcript of my interview with Lou Waters on CNN.

CNN Today

Economist Allen Smith Discusses 'The Alleged Budget Surplus, Social Security & Voodoo Economics'

Aired September 27, 2000 - 2:01 p.m. ET

LOU WATERS, CNN ANCHOR: You know that old song "We're in the Money"? You might hear a few Washington politicians humming that tune today. Thanks to a well-greased economic machine that, like that battery-powered bunny, just keeps on ticking.

The federal government is ending the fiscal year this week flush with cash, apparently, $230 billion in surplus, the largest surplus in U.S. history. President Clinton did a little election-year crowing, mentioning Al Gore by name at least twice as he ran down the numbers. Mr. Clinton says $223 billion of the surplus went toward the national debt, and he says there's something in that for you. Like we said, it's an election year.

(BEGIN VIDEO CLIP)

WILLIAM J. CLINTON, PRESIDENT OF THE UNITED STATES: Paying off the debt will benefit America just as paying off credit cards benefits the average family. It frees up money for things that matter and it keeps interest rates lower. That will mean more investment, more jobs, lower mortgage payments, car payments and student loan payments.

(END VIDEO CLIP)

WATERS: Washington posted it's first surplus since the Vietnam War era. In 1998, $69 billion; almost double the next year to $124 billion; and now, in 2000, the surplus has just about doubled again to $230 billion.

The person you're about to meet might accuse the federal government of economic malpractice. He is economist Allen Smith, who says there is no surplus, that it's all a big, fat myth. His book is entitled "The Alleged Budget Surplus, Social Security & Voodoo Economics."

Dr. Smith joins us from Ft. Myers, Florida. He taught economics for 30 years, retiring from Eastern Illinois University in 1998 to write. And he wrote this book entitled, once again, "The Alleged Budget Surplus, Social Security & Voodoo Economics," all of which suggests you're not elated over President Clinton's announcement today of 19 billion more in the surplus since June.

ALLEN SMITH, AUTHOR, "THE ALLEGED BUDGET SURPLUS, SOCIAL SECURITY & VOODOO ECONOMICS": The figures released today I haven't seen, the breakdown in terms of the amount that is off budget and the amount that is on budget. But like all the other surpluses they've been talking about, most of this is Social Security money and Social Security Trust Fund. Prior to the figures released today, in the last 40 years, we had a surplus in the operating budget of seven-tenths of a billion, or 700 million, and that came in fiscal '99. Thirty-eight years prior to that, every year had a deficit in operating budget. This is Social Security money they're talking about and not general tax revenue.

WATERS: You're saying that this money that we're hearing is a government surplus that we're paying down the federal debt with is Social Security money?

SMITH: It is Social Security money and they are not paying down the national debt. If I could, I just went on the Internet to the Treasury Department's Web site and printed out -- they have a page on there -- the public debt to the penny. And they give it -- they show a public debt of two years ago, in 1998, of 5,526 billion, and today it is 5,646. According to the Treasury Department official figures, the national debt has increased by $120 billion in this two-year period in which Clinton says it's being paid down.

What they're doing is borrowing from Social Security money, paying off what they describe as the publicly held debt and trying to make the American people believe the debt's going down.

WATERS: Well, if what you say is true, what do we make of these political promises of a prescription drug benefit, preschool for all, college tuition paid for, tax cuts? We heard Al Gore just a few minutes ago saying they, meaning Republicans, would squander the surpluses. And he's talking about a tax cut.

SMITH: These are outrageous proposals, both the proposals of George W. Bush and that of Al Gore, will tend to derail the economy, as has happened so many times before. I don't know if they've consulted with any economists, if they've looked at the facts. But Al Gore has said we'll be debt-free by 2012, and you can -- anybody can go to the Internet and get this "Mid-Session Review." It's from the office of the president, the OMB, submitted to Congress in June. And the figures in here will show that President Clinton is showing an increase in the national debt between 2000 and 2012 of about close to an additional trillion dollars.

WATERS: So we're being misled by the politicians with all these campaign promises?

SMITH: We are being totally deceived. I think this is the biggest deception in American history. It started back about 10 years ago under President Bush at the time the Social Security surpluses first came into being.

I think what the American people need to know, and most don't seem to know, and I don't hear it anyplace in the news, is the so-called "surplus" all originated as a result of legislation passed in 1983 in reaction to a presidential commission headed by Alan Greenspan in 1982 which indicated we were going to have major problems with Social Security when the baby boomers retired, beginning about 2010.

So they took action, they raised tax rates and the sort. Every bit of this surplus is a planned surplus and it is in the Social Security. I don't know the figures today, but as of last year, the only surplus that was not in Social Security was seven-tenths of a billion, or 700 million. And we have spent 4,600 billion of red ink in the last 20 years.

WATERS: I would certainly agree with you we're not hearing any of this in the news. I'm involved in the news. Are you a voice crying in the wilderness? And if not, why haven't we seen a presidential candidate, any presidential candidate, talk about this?

SMITH: I think because -- there's one of -- there's only two explanations. One, they don't know the facts, they don't know anything. The other is, they're deliberately misleading the American people. And I think it's the latter. George W. Bush's early proposal for the massive tax cut, that was just an unthinkable -- that's more Reaganomics. It's exactly the same thing Ronald Reagan said. And when Ronald Reagan came into office, we had accumulated $1 trillion in debt. We now have 5.6 trillion; 4.6 trillion of that, or 82 percent, has come under Clinton, Bush and Reagan. And the American people seem to be of the impression that we don't have a debt because of the lack of a current deficit.

WATERS: I can hear boomers now. There are between 70 and 80 million of them saying if the Social Security surplus is being used to pay down the debt, what about my Social Security?

SMITH: Well, not only that, the Social Security money has all been used for general operating purposes since it first came out back in the early -- or the late '80s. President Bush, at the time he was in office, he said, "read my lips: no new taxes," and yet he spent a substantial amount of the increased revenue from Social Security, the surplus that came along. Sen. Daniel Moynihan, at that time, actually suggested that we repeal that Social Security tax increase to keep them from getting it.

So we started back in the Bush administration pulling the wool over the American people's eyes, and it's been going on ever since.

WATERS: Is there a danger for the future?

SMITH: There is a big danger because our economy right now is healthy, extremely healthy, but the budget of the United States government is probably the worst it's ever been in terms of indebtedness, and any actions taken by the government does have an impact on the economy. And I think that either -- the plans of either of the two candidates will derail this economy and put us back into recession and major problems.

WATERS: But we all thought, because of the economy, because of more jobs, because of more people working and paying taxes and corporate profits up, corporate taxes up, that that's the reason why we have these surpluses.

SMITH: No.

WATERS: No.

SMITH: That is -- the reason is the result of the 1983 tax increase. It is the reason that we had the tiny surplus last year. And probably, of the amount announced today, when they release the figures, they'll tell us how much of that 230 billion is in the Social Security fund and how much is in the general operating budget. My guess is there's not more than 30 billion there.

And we would expect that to be the case when the economy's at a point with the lowest unemployment in 30 years, but it won't continue. Recessions always follow expansions and we will be back in deficit territory before very long whether we have any tax cuts or not. And the tax cuts will just make it worse.

WATERS: A dire warning from economist Allen Smith. Thank you, Professor, for joining us today.

SMITH: Thank you for having me.

WATERS: The book: "The Alleged Budget Surplus, Social Security & Voodoo Economics."

I was only one of many economists trying to alert the public to the "budget-surplus myth," months before President George W. Bush was even elected. Once Bush's election was certain, many economists tried to warn the public that his massive proposed tax cut would be disastrous for both the budget and the economy. But nobody wanted to listen to professional economists when their President was insisting that there was surplus money, and promising to give some of it back to them.

At the time of Bush's State of the Union address, the United States Government owed approximately $5 trillion dollars more than it had owed just 20 years earlier when President Reagan had taken office. This represented $5 trillion of unpaid bills. Bush's own father had contributed greatly to this massive red-ink spending. During George H.W. Bush's four years as president, the on-budget deficit (excluding Social Security funds) averaged more than $286 billion per year. And when he left office, the national debt that had been only $1 trillion at the beginning of the Reagan-Bush administration had soared above the $4 trillion mark!

President Clinton also ran on-budget deficits during the first six years of his presidency. However, because of the Clinton deficit-reduction package, the deficits declined significantly during each of Clinton's first six years. Finally, in 1999, the deficit was totally eliminated, and there was a tiny surplus of $1.9 billion. In fiscal 2000, the federal budget had a surplus of $86.6 billion. These were the only two non-Social Security surpluses during the preceding 40-year period, and they may well prove to be the only two surpluses that many Americans will see during their entire lifetimes.

The budget returned to deficit territory during George W. Bush's first year in office, posting an on-budget deficit of $32.5 billion in fiscal 2001. The deficit soared to $317.5 billion in 2002, $538.4 billion in 2003, and $567.4 billion in 2004. Thus, instead of paying down the debt as promised, President Bush added approximately as much to the debt in 2 years as was added during the first 200 years of American history. The deficits are projected to remain in the $500 billion plus range indefinitely unless action is taken to reduce them, and I see no deficit-reduction plans on the horizon.

George W. Bush should have been in a better position than almost anyone else to know just how dire the federal budget situation was and what a dismal failure Reaganomics had been during the 12 years Reagan and Bush were in office. His father was vice president for eight years under Reagan, and served four years as president. As the son of the vice president for eight years, and as the son of the president of the United States for four years, George W. Bush had access to information not available to many.

With aspirations to be president himself someday, the younger Bush must have talked shop with his father and tried to learn as much about the job as possible. Certainly he had to know that during those 12 years of Reagan and Bush, the national debt had quadrupled. Didn't he have any concern that Ronald Reagan and the elder Bush had added three times as much to the national debt in just 12 years as all the previous presidents in American history had added in nearly 200 years?

He must have shared his father's pain when the elder Bush failed to win reelection. And all he had to do to learn why his father had been defeated was listen to the news. It was the economy and the massive deficits that did his father in, and it was Clinton's promise to reduce the deficits that brought victory to him.   Knowing about those massive deficits during the Reagan-Bush years, and knowing how much the national debt had risen in just a few years, how could George W. Bush keep a straight face when he told the American people that the government had surplus money?

There was no surplus money except for the Social Security fund, and Bush pledged not to touch that money. As for the surpluses in 1999 and 2000, during the Clinton administration, they weren't enough to even offset the 1997 deficit of $103.4 billion, let alone the other Clinton deficits. The surpluses of 1999 and 2000 came at the peak of the business cycle when the economy was in overdrive, and the unemployment rate was at a 30-year low. Only under such conditions did the economy have the potential to generate enough revenue to even balance the budget. And let's remember that those two years were preceded by 38 consecutive years of deficits.

So where in the world did President Bush think there was going to be surplus revenue? The surpluses in the Social Security fund, that would last only a few more years before turning into deficits, were specifically earmarked for payment of the increased benefits that would coincide with the retirement of the baby boomers. And, once again, Bush had pledged that the Social Security surpluses would be placed in a lockbox not to be used for anything but the payment of Social Security benefits.

There was no way that there could be ongoing surpluses in the non-Social Security budget, as Bush learned when he ran a budget deficit during his very first year in office. The tax structure was barely capable of generating enough revenue to balance the budget in the top phase of the business cycle when all resources were employed and the economy was producing at its maximum capacity. Only rarely, and for short periods of time, is the economy at this stage. At all other times, the economy is either in recession or in the process of recovering from the last recession. During such times, the economy is not operating at the full-employment level, and experience over the previous 40 years had shown that in most years there would be at least a small deficit.

Despite these facts, President Bush told the nation that the government had massive surpluses. He does not use qualifying words such as "projected surplus" or "anticipated surplus." He talks of the surplus as if he already had it locked in a vault. Consider the following statement:

"We have increased our budget at a responsible 4 percent. We have funded our priorities. We paid down all the available debt. We have prepared for contingencies. And we still have money left over."

George W. Bush was talking about make-believe money, but he led his audience to believe that it was the real thing. He and his staff had concocted a make-believe, fantasy-land budget, and they had manipulated the numbers in such a way as to create make-believe surpluses.

Bush had not yet done any of the things he refers to. Certainly he had not paid down any of the national debt. On the contrary, he would add more than a trillion dollars to the national debt within four years. He would break the lock on the Social Security lockbox during his very first year, and, during his second year, he would still not have enough money to pay the bills after spending all of the Social Security money. And there would never be any money left over, not even play money.

He explains the reason for the nonexistent surplus as follows:

"The growing surplus exists because taxes are too high and government is charging more than it needs. The people of America have been overcharged and, on their behalf, I am here asking for a refund."

There was no growing surplus, except for the temporary, planned Social Security surplus. The non-Social Security budget had consistently run deficits for four decades except for 1999 and 2000. How could Bush say that the government was charging more in taxes than it needed when his own father had run an average non-Social Security deficit of more than $286 billion per year during his four years as President, and President Clinton had run deficits during 6 of his 8 years as President?

President George W. Bush, who was asking for the trust and support of the American people, deliberately deceived them during his very first State of the Union address. He did so in order to pass a massive tax cut that he knew was not in the best interest of the nation or the economy. It was political payback time. Those wealthy supporters who had given so much money to Bush's campaign had to be repaid. Otherwise, they might not be so generous when he ran for a second term.

In addition to misrepresenting the financial status of the federal budget, Bush also misrepresented the potential economic effects of his proposed tax cut. On February 8, 2001, in an effort to stampede his tax cut through Congress, Bush suggested that the economy was headed for trouble that his tax cut could prevent. Speaking at a Rose Garden ceremony, Bush said, "A warning light is flashing on the dashboard of our economy. And we can't just drive on and hope for the best. We must act without delay." The president said his 10-year, $1.6 trillion tax cut proposal would "jump-start the economy," and he argued that swift passage of his plan by Congress could make the difference between growth and recession.

Many observers were shocked that a new president, who had been in office less than three weeks, would make such an irresponsible statement and risk spooking the markets and lowering consumer confidence. When Roosevelt became President during the depth of the Great Depression, he said, "The only thing we have to fear is fear itself," in an effort to calm the public and build optimism. The fields of economics and psychology are so interwoven that if enough Americans come to believe that the nation is about to enter into a recession, their behavior will actually cause a recession. People will respond to their fears by cutting back on spending in preparation for anticipated layoffs, and as new orders to factories begin to decline, workers will indeed be laid off.

To use such scare tactics to get a tax cut, which does little to stimulate the economy, enacted is inexcusable for any President. Some observers suggested that Bush also had another reason for making the statement. After the longest economic expansion in American history, during the Clinton presidency, it seemed almost a certainty that a recession would occur some time during President Bush's four years in office. Some accused Bush of trying to speed up the recession so that the economy would have gone through the recession and recovered by the time he had to run for a second term. No matter what the motives, there is little question that Bush's reckless statement did contribute, at least in a small way, to the recession.

The other flaw in his argument was that quick passage of his tax cut would stimulate the economy. Bush's original proposal did little to provide short-term stimulus. To stimulate the economy in the short-term, you must put money into the hands of those consumers who will spend it. Tax cuts to the very rich results in little or no new consumer spending because the rich already have sufficient purchasing power to buy whatever they need.

CHAPTER FIVE

The Plot to Destroy Social Security

As we contemplate basic reform of the Social Security system, we would do well to draw a few lessons from the Leninist strategy...we must first prepare the political ground...First we must recognize that there is a firm coalition behind the present Social Security system...we must begin to divide this coalition and cast doubt on the picture of reality it presents to the general public. Second we must recognize that we need more than a manifesto...What we must do is construct a coalition around the Ferrara plan...That coalition should consist of not only those who will reap benefits from the IRA-based private system...but also the banks, insurance companies, and other institutions that will gain...

--Cato Journal, vol 3., no. 2 (Fall 1983)

    The playbook, upon which President Bush's strategy for privatizing Social Security is based, was written in 1983 by Stuart Butler (a Cato director) and Peter Germanis (a policy analyst at the Heritage Foundation) and published in the *Cato Journal, vol. 3, no.2 (Fall 1983).* Excerpts from the plan, which was titled, "ACHIEVING A 'LENINIST' STRAGEGY," are reproduced above.

The article, outlining the plot, begins with a comparison of the views of Marx and Lenin with regard to the belief that capitalism was doomed by its inherent contradictions. According to Butler and Germanis, Marx believed that capitalism would inevitably collapse on its own. However, Lenin wanted to mobilize an alliance, both to hasten the collapse and to ensure that the result conformed with his interpretation of the proletarian state. Butler and Germanis state that, *"Unlike many other socialists at the time, Lenin recognized that fundamental change is contingent both upon a movement's ability to create a focused political coalition and upon its success in isolating and weakening its opponents".*

Butler and Germanis urged the adoption of a similar strategy for reforming Social Security. They write, *"As we contemplate basic reform of the Social Security system, we would do well to draw a few lessons from the Leninist strategy. Many critics of the present system believe, as Marx and Lenin did of capitalism, that the system's days are numbered because of its contradictory objectives of attempting to provide both welfare and insurance. All that really needs to be done, they contend, is to point out these inherent flaws to the taxpayers and to show them that Social Security would be vastly improved if it were restructured into a predominantly private system."*

The authors argue that, "*It will be a long time before citizen indignation will cause radical change to take place.   Therefore, if we are to achieve basic changes in the system, we must first prepare the political ground so that the fiasco of the last 18 months is not repeated.*" Here the authors are referring to the lack of success of the conservatives in getting privatization included as part of the 1983 Social Security "fix."

Butler and Germanis advocate a specific set of plans for accomplishing the goal of replacing the existing Social Security system with a private system. They write, "*By approaching the problem in this way, we may be ready for the next crisis in Social Security—ready with a strong coalition for change, a weakened coalition supporting the current system, and a general public familiar with the private-sector option.*"

All the elements of the current Bush crusade are spelled out in the 1983 playbook, or "plot book." Under the heading of, A Plan of Action, the following recommendations are made:

1.) We will meet the next financial crisis in Social Security with a private alternative ready in the wings—an alternative with which the public is familiar and comfortable, and one that has the backing of a powerful political force."

2.) The second main element in our reform strategy involves what one might crudely call guerrilla warfare against both the current Social Security system and the coalition that supports it."

3.) Building a constituency for Social Security reform requires mobilizing the various coalitions that stand to benefit from the change. Such a constituency is already extensive, but mobilizing it could become a self-generating process...The business community, and financial institutions in particular, would be an obvious element in the constituency. Not only does business have a great deal to gain from a reform effort designed to stimulate private savings, but it also has the power to be politically influential and to be instrumental in mounting a public education campaign."

4.) The final element of the strategy must be to propose moving to a private Social Security system in such as way as to detach, or at least neutralize, segments of the coalition that supports the existing system. A necessary step toward this objective is to honor all outstanding claims on the current system. Without such a commitment, we can never overcome the political opposition to reform, because the retired (or nearly retired) population will continue to strongly oppose any package that threatens to significantly reduce their benefits."

It is clear that the Bush administration is going by the book of the Cato Institute. Every element of the Bush strategy is an exact match for the recommendations that were published in the Cato Journal in 1983 under the title, "Achieving A 'Leninist' Strategy."

The Cato plot against Social Security was written three years before George W. Bush sold his failing oil company and did some real soul searching as to what he should do with his life. Although he had worked on his father's political campaigns, he had not sought any other political office for himself since his 1978 unsuccessful run for Congress. But he was now thinking about a possible political career. He would consider running for governor of Texas. Even at that early stage of Bush's political career, the plot to destroy Social Security was already three years old and waiting for a president who would adopt it as his own plan someday.

The final paragraph of "Achieving a 'Leninist' Strategy," illustrates the resolve and determination by the conservatives to someday completely dismantle the Social Security program and replace it with a privatized system. It reads, *"Finally, we must be prepared for a long campaign. The next Social Security crisis may be further away than many people believe. Or perhaps it will occur before the reform coalition is strong enough to achieve a political breakthrough. In either case, it could be many years before the conditions are such that a radical reform of Social Security is possible. But then, as Lenin well knew, to be a successful revolutionary, one must also be patient and consistently plan for real reform."*

These revolutionaries must have been very disappointed that the 1983 Social Security "fix" worked as well as it did. They apparently got tired of waiting for a real Social Security crisis to come along and decided to convince George W. Bush to create such a crisis.

The building of a constituency for Social Security reform, by mobilizing the various coalitions that stand to benefit from the change that the playbook called for, has been accomplished. Thomas B. Edsall of the Washington Post wrote an excellent article titled, "Conservatives Join Forces for Bush Plans," that appeared in the February 13, 2005 issue of the Post

Edsall writes, "Recognizing the wariness of other conservatives to tackle Social Security, Cato in 1983 published an article calling for privatization of the system. The article argued that companies that stand to profit from privatization—'the banks, insurance companies and other institutions that will gain'—had to be brought into alliance. Second, the article called for initiation of "guerrilla warfare against both the current Social Security system and the coalition that supports it."

"Just 22 years later," Edsall continues, "the business alliance is fully on board in the drive to create partially private social Security accounts. The campaign is being funded largely with money set aside by major corporations to influence the outcome of the congressional debate. The money will go for lobbying, television advertising, grass-roots campaigning, letter-writing and phone calls in a bid to win majorities in the Republican-controlled House and Senate."

The number of conservative organizations supporting the privatization of Social Security, and the size of their bankroll for accomplishing the mission, is staggering. In addition to the leading proponent, the Cato Institute, other members of the coalition include, the Heritage Foundation, the National Center for Policy Analysis, the American Legislative Exchange Council, and such advocacy groups as the Club for Growth, Progress for America, FreedomWorks, Americans for Tax Reform, and the Free Enterprise Fund. (Source: Thomas B. Edsall, Washington Post.)

Edsall quotes Edwin J. Feulner, president of the Heritage Foundation, as saying, "Conservatives intend to fix Social Security, welfare and Medicare—the very problems that liberals created. And we'll do so no matter how often the lefts yells, 'Stop!'"

According to Edsall, "With billions of dollars at stake, a large network of influential conservative groups is mounting a high-priced campaign to help the White House win passage of legislation to partially privatize Social Security and limit class-action lawsuits.

"Corporate America, the financial services industry, conservative think tanks, much of the Washington trade association community, The Republican Party and GOP lobbyists and consultants are prepared to spend $200 million or more to influence the outcome of two of the touchiest legislative fights in recent memory."

According to Edsall, "This diverse coalition is bound by economic, ideological and partisan concerns. Many of the groups, for instance, are staunch advocates of free-market policies and reducing dependence on government...What's more, Wall Street and the financial sector stand to reap substantial fees from the management of personal Social Security accounts. "

Such a constituency is already extensive, but mobilizing it could become a self-generating process...The business community, and financial institutions in particular, would be an obvious element in the constituency. Not only does business have a great deal to gain from a reform effort designed to stimulate private savings, but it also has the power to be politically influential and to be instrumental in mounting a public education campaign."

Of course, the Cato Institute and other conservatives will never be satisfied with just the partial privatization that Bush is now advocating. They want to privatize the entire Social Security system.

The list of principles for Social Security reform on Cato's website includes the following statement.

"You don't cut out half a cancer. Given the advantages of a funded Social Security system, there is no excuse for stopping at only 2-3 percent of payroll taxes. Once Congress has conceded that individual capital investment can provide better and more secure retirement benefits, it should press on and allow workers to control the maximum feasible amount of their retirement income".

Once you understand the Cato Institute plan for privatizing Social Security, which Bush is trying to sell as his own plan, Bush's seemingly futile continuing road campaign makes a lot more sense. At this stage of the game, Bush doesn't care how many people support his call for privatization. His primary goal at this time is to convince the American public that Social Security does face serious problems and that some kind of reform is needed. Bush does not care nearly as much about his success in convincing Americans that privatization is the best answer to Social Security's problems as he does about convincing the public that some kind of Social Security reform is necessary.

The goal at this point is to get the public to accept the notion that there is something wrong with the current Social Security program. Bush likes to say that it was fine for the time when it was created 70 years ago, but that we need major reform and modernization of the program. Although public opinion polls show that there is not strong public support for Bush's privatization proposal, his campaign to convince the public that there is a real Social Security problem is gaining momentum.

Point number one of the Cato game plan for privatizing Social Security that was discussed earlier in this chapter states, "First we must recognize that there is a firm coalition behind the present Social Security system...Before Social Security can be reformed, we must begin to divide this coalition and cast doubt on the picture of reality it presents to the general public." The plan also called for initiation of "guerrilla warfare against both the current Social Security system and the coalition that supports it.."

President Bush and his fellow conservatives have certainly been following the strategy set down in 1983 Cato plan. They have certainly done everything in their power to "cast doubt on the picture of reality" that supporters of the current Social Security program presents to the general public, and they have been engaged in guerrilla warfare against the current Social Security program and everyone who supports it.

If the public can be convinced that Social Security is in deep trouble and needs a major overhaul, the conservatives will have won a major battle in their war against Social Security. They will then turn their attention to convincing the public that privatization is the best way to solve Social Security's problems, and they will argue for full privatization instead of just partial privatization.

Of course, Social Security is not facing any imminent crisis. The claims that Social Security is going to go flat bust, broke or bankrupt are lies. So far nobody has proposed repealing the payroll tax that is the source of Social Security revenue. The payroll tax has generated more revenue than was needed for benefit payments every year since 1984, and it will continue to do so until at least 2017. Then, after 33 consecutive years of Social Security surpluses, Social Security will begin to run deficits at some point around 2017.

However, if the money that is supposed to be in the trust fund is replaced, Social Security will continue to be able to pay full benefits until at least 2041. And Social Security will not be bankrupt even in 2041. The payroll tax revenue will continue to flow in, and there will be sufficient revenue to pay approximately 74 percent of promised benefits after 2041 even if nothing is done. Receiving 74 percent of promised benefits, instead of 100 percent, may be cause for concern, but it certainly does not constitute being flat broke, bust, or bankrupt.

The conservatives and libertarians, with George W. Bush as their spokesman, have activated the "Leninist Strategy," that they first developed in 1983, precisely because they do not see any real Social Security crisis on the horizon. With the re-election of President George W. Bush, and with Republican control of the Congress, they are gambling that they can pull the wool over the eyes of the American public and pull off their revolution at this time even in the absence of a Social Security crisis.

President George W. Bush's determined effort to partially privatize Social Security is not the product of his own planning and thinking. It is the result of the efforts of the Cato Institute, the Heritage Foundation, and other conservative think tanks and organizations. They laid the foundation for implementing the strategy to destroy Social Security and replace it with private accounts. This strategy was first enunciated by Stuart Butler of the Cato Institute and Peter Germanis of the Heritage Foundation in their 1983 article, "Achieving A 'Leninist' Strategy."

The publication of this detailed plan for privatization of Social Security was the beginning of a right-wing conspiracy to use "guerrilla warfare," and other tactics modeled after Lenin's plan to overthrow capitalism, in order to kill the Social Security program, and replace it with a system of private accounts. The conservative conspiracy was based on the assumption that Social Security was such a popular program with such strong backing, that it could not be brought down through the normal democratic process where, at least in theory, the wishes of the majority of the people determine the fate of government programs.

The conspirators decided that they, a small minority of right-wing Americans who opposed government programs, could prevail over the majority of Americans who continued to support Social Security in its traditional form, by using a strategy similar to that used by Lenin to overthrow the Russian government and replace it with communism. They advocated adopting a Leninist strategy to overthrow traditional Social Security and replace it with private accounts.

There is nothing in the article about what might be best for America as a whole, or what might be fair. The conservative conspirators did not concern themselves with considerations of who might be hurt if their revolution was successful. They recognized that they needed "more than a manifesto." They argued, "What we must do is construct a coalition...that will gain directly from its implementation. That coalition should consist of not only those who will reap benefits from the IRA-based private system...but also the banks, insurance companies, and other institutions that will gain from providing such plans to the public."

The 1983 plot was clearly a declaration of war against the current Social Security program in the United States of America. But it was a lot more than that. It was a declaration of war against the American democratic system where individual Americans could theoretically decide the future of the nation through the power of their votes. The plot was clearly against the principle of majority rule.

George W. Bush may have played no direct role in formulating the right-wing plot to privatize Social Security, but it was certainly consistent with Bush's thinking at the time. Five years earlier, in his 1978 unsuccessful Congressional election campaign, Bush proposed privatization and predicted that Social Security would be bankrupt by the late 1980s. (Boston Globe, February 6, 2005 article by Richard Parker, "The pragmatist and the utopian".)

Bush embraced the privatization strategy during the 2000 campaign and won a lot of conservative support and money for doing so. But he did not push for Social Security reform during his first term, nor did he make it a very big issue in the 2004 race. It was only after he was safely elected to a second term that Bush became bold enough to join forces with other conservatives and make a determined effort to help the conservatives try to implement the strategy.

Not only has George W. Bush betrayed the trust of the American people by continuing to raid the Social Security trust fund, but he is now traveling around the country, on behalf of his conservative base trying to sell a lie.

As I have reported earlier in this book, there is nothing remotely resembling an imminent crisis facing Social Security, and Social Security will not be bankrupt in 2041, even if nothing is done. President Bush is also deliberately lying to the American people when he says he wants to "save" and "strengthen" Social Security.

You don't make Social Security stronger by tapping into the revenue flow and diverting a part of it to private accounts. You don't make Social Security stronger when you continue to raid the trust fund of more than $400 million of Social Security money per day and spend it on other programs. President Bush, like most conservatives, has always hated Social Security, and there is probably no other legacy that he would rather leave than that he was the president who killed Social Security.

CHAPTER SIX

The Invitation-Only Road Show

President Bush: *"You got any thoughts about
Social Security?"*
Christy Paavola: *"Yes. I don't think it's going to be there
when I retire, which is really scary."*
President Bush: *"Got anything else you want to say?"*

Christy Paavola: *"I really like the idea of personal savings
accounts."*
President Bush: *"You did a heck of a job. You deserve an
A."*

--Exchange between President Bush and invited stage guest Concordia
University senior Christy Paavola, at a Milwaukee "Invitation-only"
Social Security Town Hall Meeting (SOURCE: Los Angeles Times,
May 19, 2005, story by Warren Vieth)

At the beginning of March 2005, the Bush
administration used great fanfare to announce a 60-day
Social Security tour to promote Bush's privatization plan
that would include at least 60 stops. As it turned out, so
little progress was made during those 60 days, that the tour
was extended indefinitely.

Peter Baker gave a lack of progress report in the May 20, 2005 issue of the Washington Post that included the following comments.

"The obligatory campaign-style signs were hung behind the stage, the familiar hand-selected 'conversation participants' seated next to him. The friendly, invitation-only audience cheered with appropriate enthusiasm. And when President Bush took the microphone, he spun out more or less the same speech he has given dozens of times before.

"On the 78th day of a 60-day roadshow, the president's nationwide Social Security tour, even to some of his own aides, has the feel of a past-its-prime Broadway production that has been held over while other, newer shows steal the spotlight."

The Bush people tried to portray the President's tour as a series of town hall meetings, but they were anything but traditional town hall meetings. The meetings were manipulated in such a way as to give the impression that everybody agreed with Bush's views on Social Security. It is true that everyone attending these meetings did agree with Bush because those who did not agree with him were not issued tickets to these invitation-only meetings.

However, there was ample evidence that not everyone agreed with the president. The Los Angeles Times reported that, in Fargo, North Dakota, where Bush held a Social Security event in February, "more than 40 residents were placed on a "black list" of people who were not to receive tickets because they had expressed opposition to Bush's policies." (Peter Wallsten and Warren Vieth, Los Angeles Times, March 11, 2005)

In Denver, three people were forcibly removed from one of President Bush's town meetings on Social Security. They first thought they had been removed by the Secret Service and could not understand why. They had said nothing, were carrying no signs, and had been invited by

Republican Congressman, Bob Beauprez. As it turned out, the three were forced to leave by a Republican staff member, allegedly because they had a bumper sticker on their car that read "No More Blood for Oil" (Jim VandeHei, Washington Post, March 30, 2005)

An attorney for the three, Dan Recht, said the three believed their Constitutional rights were violated. Recht said, "When you are punished by not being allowed to listen to your president speak because of speech you have on your bumper sticker, that is a classic First Amendment issue."

Not only are those who don't agree with Bush's Social Security plan kept out, but certain people are recruited to say good things about the President's policy. For example, the St. Petersburg Times reports how a 27-year old Pinellas County tax assistant received an unexpected call from the White House in advance of President Bush's visit to Tampa for a Social Security town hall meeting.

Jim Browne, a registered Republican was asked what he thought about President Bush's State of the Union address from the previous night, and then they asked him what he thought about Social Security. This first call was followed by three more probing calls from the White House. Finally, Browne was invited to attend Bush's town hall meeting at the Tampa Convention Center as a special on-stage guest.

Browne shared the stage with three other handpicked Floridians during a "discussion" with Bush about the future of Social Security before an invitation-only crowd...Like the others who took the stage, Browne was full of compliments.

"I'd like to say how much I appreciate you bringing up the subject of the future of Social Security," Browne told the president. "For many of my generation, we don't anticipate the system being there for us as it stands."

This was the lead that Bush wanted, so he stopped Browne and began making his standard pitch.

As Browne got phone calls from friends and family members who saw him on TV with the president, he said he was happy to be part of the program.

"I think the whole idea of today was to have a bipartisan discussion," Browne said. "The president is open to ideas. That's the message I heard today." (Michael Van Sickler, St. Petersburg Times, February 5, 2005).

How anyone could interpret this event, or the many others like it, as a "bipartisan discussion" is beyond me. A real discussion involves more than one viewpoint. Bush's appearances are nothing more than infomercials for his own partisan agenda with the tab being picked up by American taxpayers.

"The president is engaging in political carnival," said Tom Matzzie, Washington director of MoveOn.org, an advocacy group that opposes Bush's initiative. "He's not holding town hall meetings to talk with America. He's holding staged campaign events to create the media perception he wants to create." (Los Angeles Times, March 11, 2005)

Linda Felmann of the Christian Science Monitor describes a Bush appearance in Omaha in early February as follows:

"The Omaha event had a similar structure to the others: There were the visuals—a big chart showing how the number of workers supporting each beneficiary has shrunk since 1950 from 16 to 3.3. Another graphic showed how in 2018, incoming payroll taxes will no longer cover all the promised Social Security benefits and by 2042, the system will be insolvent.

..."In this chat-show portion of the event, Bush asks every panel member to tell his or her story, which includes, of course, a conclusion that allowing younger workers to put some of their Social Security withholding into a personal retirement account, invested conservatively in stocks and bonds, is the way to go.

...."The lone heckler in the hall, who was removed, was not the only one not completely sold on Bush's plan—especially when it remains unclear how the government would fund the $1 trillion-plus transition costs and by how much the government will reduce guaranteed benefits to address the solvency issue." (Linda Feldmann, The Christian Science Monitor, February 7, 2005 edition)

When one compares the message that Bush is trying to get out through his Social Security "town hall meetings" to the strategies set forth by Butler and Germanis in their 1983, "Achieving A 'Leninist' Strategy," it becomes clear that Bush is following the Cato strategy like a roadmap. Excerpts from the Cato plan follow.

"We must press for modest changes in the laws and regulations designed to make private pension options more attractive, and we must expose the fundamental flaws and contradictions in the existing system. In do doing, we will strengthen the coalition for privatizing Social Security and we will weaken the coalition for retaining or expanding the current system. By approaching the problem in this way, we may be ready for the next crisis in Social security—ready with a strong coalition for change, a weakened coalition supporting the current system, and a general public familiar with the private-sector option.

..."An economic education campaign...must be undertaken to demonstrate the weaknesses of the existing system and to allow it to be compared accurately (and therefore unfavorably) with the private alternative...The aim is to weaken political support for the present system.

..."Interest groups concerned with Social Security reform can be divided into the young, the middle-aged working population, and the retired or those nearing retirement. Of these, the young are the most obvious constituency for reform and a natural ally for the private alternative...Clearly, an important thread running through the entire strategy is education. An education campaign is needed to gain the support of key individuals in the media as well as to win over vital constituencies for political reform." (Stuart Butler and Peter Germanis, Cato Journal, vol. 3, no. 2, Fall 1983)

The so-called "education campaign" that the strategy calls for is what Bush's Social Security tour is all about. However, he is not educating the public. He is deliberately deceiving them. The Bush tour is a propaganda campaign designed to deceive and confuse the public so they will support the privatization of Social Security.

The President of the United States is using taxpayer money to finance a campaign to destroy a 70-year-old government program which the vast majority of American's support. Public opinion polls have shown from the very beginning that the majority of Americans do not support Bush's privatization proposal. During the 2004 campaign he chose to spend more time on "moral" issues than on Social Security. He had the opportunity to make the election a referendum on his Social Security proposal, but he chose not to do so, because he would not have been re-elected if the public knew that his number one domestic goal was to destroy the Social Security program as we now know it.

The American people have sent Bush a clear message through their responses to the pollsters. They do not want privatization of Social Security. The longer Bush tours the country trying to sell his proposal, the less support there is for the program. In addition, it does not appear that the majority of the members of Congress support Bush on this issue. So why does Bush continue his campaign?

He does so because he is accomplishing the first step in the strategy laid down by Butler and Germanis in "Achieving A 'Leninist' Strategy." That first step is to "demonstrate the weaknesses of the existing system." This is part of what Butler and Germanis call, "guerrilla warfare against both the current Social Security system and the coalition that supports it."

Bush is succeeding in convincing the American people that Social Security is not totally problem free. Where there is as much smoke as Bush is generating, there must be at least a tiny fire. That is all that Bush needs to accomplish in this first stage. If he can convince Congress and the public that Social Security needs at least some minor reform, he has won the first round. It is in round two, during the Congressional debate on whatever legislation is proposed and introduced, that the real drive for privatization will take place.

President Bush is leading a movement to put the wishes of libertarians and conservatives above the wishes of Americans as a whole. He is trying to destroy the current Social Security system and replace it with private accounts. Certainly Bush and the minority of Americans who would like to see this happen have a right to express their views and try to sell them to the majority of Americans. But that is not what is going on here.

Bush and his fellow conservatives are trying to destroy the current Social Security program through a revolutionary approach first laid down in 1983. In the words of Butler and Germanis, "methods of neutralizing, buying out, or winning over key segments of the Social Security coalition must be explored and formulated into legislative initiatives. The objective of this element of strategy complements the first. The aim is to weaken political support for the present system."

President Bush and his allies are trying to circumvent the normal democratic process of public policy and find a way to impose the views of a minority on the majority. This is clearly a violation of the basic principles upon which this nation was founded, and they must not be allowed to get by with it.

CHAPTER SEVEN

Racing Toward Fiscal Disaster

Buried deep in the financial pages, telltale signs are appearing that suggest America may well be headed for a financial meltdown. In January 2004 the staff of the International Monetary Fund, who normally worry about profligate nations like Argentina, took direct aim at the United States, warning the world that we are careening toward insolvency.

--Excerpt from *Running on Empty* by Peter G. Peterson (Farrar, Straus and Giroux)

It took 192 years of our history and all the presidents from George Washington through Jimmy Carter to accumulate the first $1 trillion in national debt. Actually, the debt was $932 billion when Carter turned over the reins of government to Ronald Reagan in January 1981.

Although a trillion dollars is a significant amount, the fact that it took nearly 200 years to accumulate the first $1 trillion was somewhat comforting. There were many troubling problems facing America when Reagan became president, but the size, or rate of growth, of the national debt was not seen as one of them.

That all changed rather quickly. It took Reagan just a little more than five years to double the national debt to $2 trillion. And just during the 12 years of the Reagan-Bush administrations, the national debt quadrupled to more than $4 trillion. The large tax cuts under Reagan, which were not accompanied by matching spending cuts, put the nation on the fast track to economic disaster.

Bill Clinton defeated President Bush in 1992, primarily because of the massive deficits, the soaring national debt, and the weak economy. Through a deficit-reduction package that included both reduced government spending and higher taxes, Clinton reversed the trend. The deficits got smaller and smaller during Clinton's first six years, and the government experienced real budget surpluses in 1999 and 2000 for the first time in 40 years.

Unfortunately, the elimination of deficits by Clinton did nothing to undo the gigantic national debt that, by the time Clinton left office, had risen above the $6 trillion mark. We were spending approximately $1 billion per day just to pay the interest on the huge debt, which at that time was more than we were spending on national defense. When Clinton left office, the government owed more than a trillion dollars to the Social Security trust fund. Clinton, like his predecessor, had spent Social Security surplus funds that were supposed to be saved for the retirement of the baby boomers on general operating expenses.

The nation was far from trouble-free when Clinton left office but, if a return to deficits could be avoided, and if the debt to the Social Security trust fund could gradually be repaid, it looked like the nation just might find its way to long-term solvency. But the entire financial picture was fragile, and it would take very sound and responsible economic and budget policies over the course of the next two decades to avoid a financial calamity.

Putting George W. Bush in charge of such a difficult and delicate task was like turning a bull loose in a china shop. He came storming into office pushing for policies that were almost the exact opposite of what the economy needed. And he seemed determined to undo all the gains of the Clinton years.

Why is George W. Bush assaulting the federal budget with such vigor and determination? Why are more Americans not outraged that, during his first two years as president, he wiped out all the fiscal progress made during the previous eight years?

These questions seem almost impossible to answer. All that anyone can do is to examine the record and give an educated opinion as to why he or she thinks these things were allowed to happen. I do just that in the remainder of this chapter.

There is no dispute over the position of the vast majority of professional economists on the Bush tax cuts. They oppose them and fear that the cuts will inflict major damage to the American economy and the federal budget. Why would George W. Bush ignore the advice of the top economists in the nation, including at least ten Nobel Laureates? Would he also ignore the advice of the majority of experts in the field of medicine? Would he turn a deaf ear to the majority of military experts in the Pentagon?

It appears that Bush is trying to create a severe financial train wreck so that he can impose upon the American people his own vision of the proper role of the federal government. Texas is sometimes referred to as the low-tax, low-service state. Apparently George W. Bush intends to impose his low-tax, low-service philosophy on all of the American people, whether they want it or not. He seems to be trying to starve the government into turning its back on responsibilities it has held for decades.

Since Ronald Reagan became president in January 1981, conservatives have tried to destroy basic social programs, including what is often referred to as the social safety net. They want the federal government to provide national defense and little else. The conservatives would consider the demise of Social Security, Medicare, and Medicaid cause for celebration, and they are determined to prevent the government from ever creating a national health care system such as that of Canada and most other advanced nations.

Because there are enough Americans who are compassionate (in the true sense of the word), the conservatives have been unable to convince the majority of Americans to see things their way. If they cannot impose their values on America through the democratic process, they will slip them in through the back door.

This is the only explanation that makes any sense to me as to why George W. Bush seems so determined to move the nation toward bankruptcy. In the long run, for every dollar of permanent tax cuts, there must be a dollar's worth of service cuts. In the mind of George W. Bush, he is not cutting taxes. He is cutting services. And unless his tax cuts are later repealed, he has already preplanned the massive cutting of government programs and services.

There is nothing wrong with tax cuts so long as the federal budget is in balance and people are informed of what services they will lose as a result of a tax cut. But Bush's tax cuts were sold as unconditional gifts to the American people. Not once did I hear Bush say, "On behalf of your government I am going to give you back some money in exchange for your giving up certain services that you have become accustomed to." Instead, Bush gave the impression that there were no strings attached. He was playing Santa Claus.

Maybe I'm more suspicious than most people, but when anyone tells me they are going to "give" me some money, red flags pop up all over the place. I immediately try to figure out what they expect to get in return. And when a politician offers to give me some money, I know immediately that he is going to want something in return. But I don't think enough Americans have been asking themselves, "What are the Bush tax cuts going to cost me?"

At least they weren't asking that question prior to February 2004 when Alan Greenspan said the government would have to cut future Social

Security benefits because it had promised more than it could deliver. But a lot more Americans may have started asking the critical question after Bush's election to a second term when he began talking about the terrible financial condition of Social Security. Of course, Bush's rich friends knew all along that there was no money in the Social Security trust fund, because Mr. Bush had used the Social Security surplus to finance large income tax cuts for them.

Is it too late to avert an economic disaster and the collapse of Social Security? Like a politician, I must say yes and no. Much of the damage that has already been done is irreversible. The skyrocketing growth in the national debt from $1 trillion when Reagan took office to $7.8 trillion today cannot be reversed. That $6.8 trillion of additional debt will be with us forever. Our children, grandchildren, and all generations that come after them will have to pay interest on this mammoth debt. Furthermore, future interest payments on the debt will be much higher than current payments because interest will not remain indefinitely at current abnormally low levels.

However, a radical change in course could halt the ongoing damage and keep the national debt from soaring out of control. We must begin to handle federal finances the same way that any responsible family or business handles its finances. We must terminate the practice of spending money that we don't have.

Government spending should not exceed the amount of revenue that would be generated by the tax system if the economy were operating at the full employment level. Spending above and beyond that level is reckless and irresponsible. If increased spending is absolutely unavoidable because of an emergency such as a war, special arrangement must be made to finance the war. Either a special, temporary emergency tax must be enacted, or the money must be obtained by cutbacks in other spending programs. George W. Bush has done just the opposite. He has pushed through large tax cuts at the very time that military spending has soared. The simultaneous enactment of big tax cuts and massive increases in military spending is destructive and ruinous to the country's future.

In order to understand the origin of the Bush tax cuts, one must examine the history and motivation behind George W. Bush's run for the presidency.

When Bush's father, George H.W. Bush, was defeated by Bill Clinton in 1992, George W. resolved to avenge his father's defeat and become president himself. This was an ambitious goal for a man who had never held any political office. But George W. Bush wasn't just any man. He was the son of a United States president and a member of a powerful political family. In addition, he had access to almost unlimited money for launching a political career.

Although George W. Bush had run for Congress back in 1978, he lost that election and seemed to have also lost his taste for politics. At the time of his father's defeat for re-election in 1992, fourteen years had passed since that ill-fated run for Congress and George W. had not run for any other political office. But that soon changed.

George W. decided to run for governor of Texas in 1994. It would be tough to unseat the popular incumbent Governor Ann Richards, but Bush had access to unlimited money, and he had the brilliant political strategist Karl Rove at his side.

Bush managed to defeat Richards and become governor. Four years later, in 1998, Bush was reelected to a second term, and thus he had a launching pad for his bid for the presidency. But, aside from his wealth and family name, Bush did not have a lot going for him in terms of years of political experience or strong academic credentials. It was one thing to get elected governor, but the competition would be a lot tougher in his bid for the presidency. He needed something special to differentiate himself from others who were also seeking the presidency.

Bush was a strong admirer of Ronald Reagan's success in making it to the White House despite his lack of national political experience. Reagan had made it to the oval office because of his promise to cut taxes if he were elected. If it had worked for the former California governor, why couldn't it work for the Texas governor?

The rest is history. George W. Bush decided early in his bid for the Republican nomination that he would follow the same strategy that had taken Ronald Reagan to the White House. He would promise to enact large tax cuts if he were elected.

Bush was the only proponent of major tax cuts in a large field of candidates during the 2000 Republican presidential primaries. Given the success of Clinton's deficit reduction program that led to declining deficits during the first six years of his presidency and modest surpluses during 1999 and 2000, how could any responsible candidate propose a return to the massive deficits of the past? The answer is that no responsible candidate could or would have chosen that course.

George W. Bush, however, was not concerned about what a responsible candidate would propose. He wanted to be a successful candidate. He wanted to become the next President of the United States. If this required deviating from sound economic and fiscal policies, he was willing to pay that price.

Bush's promise to enact large tax cuts if he were elected was criticized by his primary opponents and economists alike. A return to Reaganomics was the last thing this country needed, but we got it none-the-less.

Once he was elected, there was no way that Bush would reverse his stand on tax cuts, but he had a tough time selling them to the Congress. Everybody likes lower taxes, but the huge projected budget deficits that would accompany them was real cause for concern.

Bush sold his tax cut legislation just like he is trying to sell Social Security reform. He used scare tactics. Just as his Social Security proposals are not designed to strengthen Social Security, his tax cut proposals were not designed to stimulate the economy. In order to boost the economy, money must be put into the hands of those consumers who will spend it. Bush's tax cuts were heavily weighted toward the wealthy, who will not respond to a tax cut with increased consumer spending.

By early 2003, it was quite clear that Bush's tax cuts had not brought the results that he had promised. The economy had stalled, the unemployment rate had risen to 6 percent, and 2 million jobs had been lost just since Bush took office. In addition, the non-Social Security deficit for fiscal 2002 had been a whopping $317.5 billion, and a $467.6 billion deficit was being projected for fiscal 2003. Obviously the Bush tax cut had affected the economy very differently than Bush had predicted. So what kind of medicine did the economy need in 2003? According to Bush, we needed still more tax cuts, so in early 2003 he called for a large new tax-cut package.

When more than 400 of the nation's top economists placed a full-page ad in the *New York Times* to warn the public about the dangers of such action, President Bush totally ignored their warnings and campaigned against them and anyone else who opposed his latest tax cut. He also traveled around the country trying to convince the American people to put pressure on Congress to pass his proposal.

In the years to come, historians will almost certainly have difficulty explaining the action of the Senate on Friday, May 23, 2003. On that date, the Senate voted to raise the nation's debt limit by nearly $1 trillion, less than a week before the Treasury Department was expected to run out of borrowing authority and risk default on the nation's debt.

What was so extraordinary about the May 23, 2003, vote to raise the debt ceiling was the fact that it came on the very same day that the Senate also passed a $350 billion tax cut. If the financial condition of the United States government was so dire as to require almost a trillion-dollar increase in the debt ceiling, how in the world could a single senator justify voting for a $350 billion tax cut?

The tax cut of 2003 was the second Trojan horse that President Bush had given to the American public. His 2001 tax-cut package was based on the myth that the federal government had huge budget surpluses with which to pay for the tax cuts. He promised that his 2001 cuts would not bring a return of deficits and that Social Security money would not be used to pay for them. Since Bush had already been proven wrong about the surplus, the return to deficits, and the borrowing of Social Security surpluses, by 2003, he could no longer use that argument . Instead, in 2003, Bush pushed through a tax cut primarily benefiting the wealthy, masquerading as a "jobs creation" bill.

In short, the Bush tax cuts, without matching spending cuts, are the primary engine propelling the government, the nation, and the American people toward the cliff of fiscal disaster. They were never affordable and were sold under false pretenses. They have served George W. Bush well and brought great benefit to his political base which he has described as "the haves and the have mores." They enabled a man who had failed at business, been rejected by the University of Texas Law School, and held only one previous elective office to become President of the United States. The tax cuts have been very good for George W. Bush and his political base, but they have been very bad for the rest of America.

This is not to say that tax cuts per se are bad. Through our democratic process, the American people should decide how much government they want and are willing to pay for. Then taxes should be just high enough to pay the bills. If the people want lower taxes, then they must be willing to accept a reduction in services. If they want additional services, then they must be willing to pay higher taxes.

The one indisputable principle of government finance is that, just like individuals and businesses, the government cannot continue to spend a great deal more than it collects in tax revenue over the long run.

CHAPTER EIGHT

Saving Social Security for Posterity

Let the people know the truth and the country is safe.

--Abraham Lincoln

Social Security, the most successful and most popular program ever created by the United States government, has lifted millions of Americans out of poverty and made their final years tolerable, if not golden. It has worked well for the past 70 years, and it can work well in perpetuity, if it is put on, and kept on, a solid foundation. Those people who dislike Social Security do so for ideological and political reasons—not because the program is unworkable or unsustainable.

Milton Friedman, the idol of conservatives and libertarians, first advocated the abolition of Social Security in 1962, with the publication of "Capitalism and Freedom." He did so, "not because the program was going bankrupt, but because he considered it immoral." reports Carolyn Lochhead in the June 5, 2005 edition of the San Francisco Chronicle.

Lochhead quotes Michael Tanner of the Cato Institute as saying, "President Bush's proposal to incorporate private accounts in the giant retirement program is easily traced to Friedman. He's the originator of it and all the discussion can be traced back to him."

At age 92, Friedman is still singing the same song he was singing 43 years ago. However, the choir is much larger today. According to Lochhead, in a recent interview at his home in San Francisco, Friedman said, "I've always been opposed to Social Security. I think it's a very unethical program."

I don't believe that Friedman's moral and ethical values are representative of those of the majority of Americans, whom I think would find a deliberate attempt to destroy Social Security unethical and immoral. Yet, that is the reason he gives for opposing Social Security. Friedman, like his fellow libertarians, does not believe the government should be involved in social programs. They oppose most government programs other than national defense, and Social Security is one of those programs they have been out to destroy for decades.

There is nothing fundamentally wrong with the current structure of the Social Security program. It is being used as a scapegoat, along with the baby-boom generation, for the unbelievably irresponsible and fraudulent fiscal policies of the United States Government. The current funding problems with Social Security are the result of the government's embezzlement of Social Security surplus funds for more than two decades.

From the enactment of the 1983 payroll tax increase to this very day, America's political leaders (both Democrats and Republicans) have spent every penny of surplus Social Security revenue on other government programs, leaving the trust fund continuously empty.   Under the leadership of President George W. Bush, the government is continuing to steal Social Security surplus money each and every day and spend it on everything from funding the income tax cuts for the rich to financing the War in Iraq.

The payroll tax increase that was part of the 1983 Social Security Amendments was designed for the explicit purpose of generating enough surplus revenue between 1984 and whenever Social Security began to run deficits to pay full benefits for decades after the surpluses ended.   There should today be approximately $1.7 trillion in real assets in the trust fund, and this amount should grow to $3.7 trillion by 2017 when the surpluses end and deficits begin.

So why does President Bush continue to say the trust fund holds nothing but empty promises and worthless IOUs?   He says this because he knows better than anyone that his father, President Clinton, and he have spent every penny of the $1.7 trillion of Social Security surplus revenue on other government programs.   President Bush also knows that, as he lies to the American people about wanting to "save" and "strengthen" Social Security, the government is continuing to raid the Social Security trust fund to the tune of more than $400 million each and every day, guaranteeing that the trust fund will remain empty.

Despite the claims and counter claims of various groups and individuals, President Bush is correct when he says there are no real assets in the trust fund. He is also correct when he says that beginning in 2017 when Social Security begins to run annual deficits after 33 consecutive years of surpluses it will not be able to pay full benefits unless the government raises taxes, borrows additional amounts from the public, or cuts government spending. But he is correct ONLY IF the American people allow him and other government officials to continue to get away with grand theft.

President Bush has the executive authority to instruct the Secretary of the Treasury to immediately stop raiding the trust fund and to invest all future Social Security surpluses in public issue marketable Treasury bonds instead of spending the money and issuing the worthless special issue government IOUs.

If the president would take this simple "stroke-of-the-pen" action, and his successors would do the same, the trust fund would begin to accumulate real assets at the rate of about $150 billion per year, and the trust fund would hold at least $2 trillion in 2017 when Social Security goes from annual surpluses to annual deficits. This $2 trillion that would be accumulated in the trust fund between now and 2017 if the government would only obey federal law, would be sufficient to supplement payroll tax revenue and enable the payment of full Social Security benefits for years. If the government would pay back the $1.7 trillion in Social Security money that it has already spent, then full Social Security benefits could be paid until at least 2041.

The main point of confusion on this whole matter seems to be that most people don't understand that public issue marketable Treasury bonds are something very different from the non-marketable special issue government IOUs that are held by the Social Security trust fund. By law, the Social Security surplus is supposed to be invested only in securities backed by "the full faith and credit of the United States Government. Currently the Treasury has only two options that meet the letter of the law. The first option is to invest the Social Security surplus in public issue marketable Treasury bonds purchased in the open market from the public. These are the type of Treasury bonds held by Japanese pension funds, the Chinese government, Bill Gates, and every other private investor who owns United States Treasury bonds.

Let's look at an example of how this would work. Suppose that Bill Gates decides to sell $10 million of his U.S. Treasury bond holdings in the open market in order to raise capital for expansion. Now suppose that the Social Security trustees use $10 million of Social Security surplus to buy public issue marketable Treasury bonds in the open market and, just by chance, end up with the bonds that Bill Gates sold. The net effect is that 10 million surplus Social Security dollars end up in the hands of Bill Gates, and the Social Security trust fund ends up with $10 million of good-as-gold marketable Treasury bonds that it can resell in the open market any time that it needs to raise money with which to pay benefits. None of this $10 million is available for President Bush and Congress to spend because it is all truly invested in real assets. It earns real interest, and the Treasury bonds can be resold in the open market at any time.

Now let's look at what really happened to that $10 million, and every other dollar of the $1.7 trillion that is supposed to be in the trust fund. The government took the money and spent it just as if it were general fund revenue.

Money can be spent, or it can be saved and invested. But once money is spent, there is nothing left to invest. Not a single dollar of the trust fund money has been invested in anything. It was taken and spent, pure and simple. The IOUs in the trust fund are simply an accounting record of how much money the government took. They do not represent money that was saved and invested, because none of the money was saved and invested. It was all spent.

We can say that the government just borrowed the money, but the word "borrowing" implies repayment. The government has been taking and spending this money for the past 22 years, and absolutely no provisions have been made for repayment of any of it. The government has neither enacted future tax increases that are scheduled to kick in when the money needs to be repaid, nor has it targeted any specific government spending programs that are scheduled to be eliminated whenever repayment of the "borrowed" Social Security money becomes necessary. Until and unless provisions have been made for repaying the "borrowed" money, I think it is appropriate to think of the money as stolen.

Suppose it is discovered that a bank employee has been taking money from the bank for 22 years, and altering the books to cover up his actions. If the employee insists that he just "borrowed" the money and plans to repay it in some way at some unknown time in the future, will the law consider him to be guilty of only borrowing the money, or will he be charged with embezzlement? He will be charged with embezzlement because he took money that did not belong to him and spent it as if it were his own.

Isn't this what the federal government has done? Hasn't it taken money that was collected specifically for the Social Security program and spent it on programs for which the money was not intended? Indeed it has. The federal government has used fraudulent accounting practices to divert the money from Social Security into other programs without the public's knowledge or consent. The government has embezzled $1.7 trillion of Social Security money, and it continues to embezzle every dollar (more than $400 million) of the Social Security surplus that flows in on a daily basis.

How has the government managed to pull off this crime? It has done so by creating a special type of government document that meets the letter of the law, but not the spirit. When the government spends Social Security money it replaces the money with pieces of paper called non-marketable special issue bonds. These so-called "bonds" have written on their face, "Backed by the full faith and credit of the United States government." This fulfills the legal requirement that Social Security funds be held only in the form of instruments backed by the full faith and credit of the government.   However, it does not meet the spirit of the law.

These special issue IOUs are available to, and held only by, the government trust funds.   They are not marketable and therefore cannot be bought or sold in the market.   They are not real assets, and they have no market value.   They could not be sold to anyone even for a penny on the dollar.   The special issue IOU's cannot be used to raise funds for Social Security benefit payments.   They serve only as an accounting record of how much Social Security money has been spent by the government on other programs.

Will the government repay the Social Security money that it has spent, and thus enable Social Security to pay full benefits until 2041 as planned?   Some people react to this question as not even worthy of an answer.   "Of course the government will repay the money," they say.   "The United States government always pays its debts."

But it is not quite that cut and dried.   The financial outlook for the federal budget is the bleakest it has ever been, and the public has been conditioned for the past 25 years to think of tax increases as just about the worst of all conceivable sins.

Currently, the government is increasing the national debt at the rate of about $1 trillion every two years.   In dollar terms, that is as much as was added to the public debt during the first 200 years of American history, and interest payments on the public debt are running more than $1 billion per day.   Finally, there is a great deal of uncertainty as to how much money will be required for the war in Iraq over the long haul.

Americans have never liked paying taxes, but at least they reluctantly supported enough taxation to meet the nation's needs prior to the Reagan presidency. Reagan convinced the people that they were being overtaxed and pushed through huge tax cuts that gave birth to years of record deficits and a skyrocketing national debt. Clinton's deficit-reduction package squeaked through the Congress without a single Republican vote, and the tax increase portion of the package was portrayed as just about the most evil thing any president could possibly do.

Under Clinton, the deficits became smaller and smaller during the first six years, and there were modest surpluses in 1999 and 2000—the first surpluses in 38 years. However, George W. Bush once again told the American people that they were being overtaxed and pushed through massive new tax cuts. Is it any wonder that many Americans believe that all tax cuts are good and all tax increases are the greatest of sins?

The government cannot repay the Social Security money without raising taxes, and I'm not sure that it will be politically feasible to raise taxes when the need arises. So instead of asking "Will the government repay the Social Security money?" perhaps we should be asking "Can the government repay the Social Security money?"

I think a strong case can be made that the government will ultimately default on its debt to Social Security. I am well aware that many people argue that the government will never default on any of its debt, because doing so would have a catastrophic impact on world financial markets.

I agree that the government can never, and will never, default on its general debt to the American public and the outside world. This debt is represented by the public issue, marketable Treasury bonds that are held by investors around the world. These marketable Treasury bonds are good-as-gold and default-proof, so no investor holding such bonds has anything to worry about. Unfortunately, none of the Social Security surplus revenue was invested in such bonds.

The special issue IOUs are an ethical and legal debt of the United States government, but the government has the Constitutional power to declare that debt null and void. Since the special issue IOUs are held only by the United States government trust funds, the government could default on this special category of debt without defaulting on any of its other debt. The outside world might frown on such action, but I think they would view it as primarily an internal political matter between the United States government and its citizens.

So we cannot rule out the possibility of a government default as long as the government has the power to do so. Steps can and should be taken to make the government's debt to Social Security default proof. The first step would be for the government to stop raiding the trust fund and invest all future Social Security surplus revenue in marketable Treasury bonds purchased in the open market. The second step would be for the government to borrow $1.7 trillion from the public and pay off its current debt to Social Security. That money would then be invested in marketable Treasury bonds purchased in the open market.

This would not result in an increase in the total debt because the increased debt to the public would be offset by the decreased debt to Social Security. It would, however, increase the amount of default-proof debt by $1.7 trillion. The net effect of these transactions would be to redeem the special issue IOUs and replace them with marketable Treasury bonds which the government could never default on.

If this all sounds so simple that you can't understand why the government has not already taken such action, please allow me to explain the down side from the viewpoint of President Bush and Congress. The Social Security surplus has been serving as a giant slush fund for the past two decades. If the government were to stop stealing from the trust fund, it would have approximately $150 billion less per year to spend than it currently has. This would necessitate major cuts in spending and/or higher taxes.

The reason that Bush broke his promise to not raid the trust fund was that, if he had kept that promise, he would have been unable to keep his promise to his rich friends that he would cut their taxes. There has never been any budget surplus, except for the Social Security surplus, since Bush became president. Therefore, he chose to use the Social Security surplus to fund his income tax cut. If he were prevented from continuing to spend the Social Security surplus, he would probably have to roll back at least part of the tax cut.

The surplus Social Security money should have been invested in pre-existing marketable Treasury bonds purchased in the open market. This would have had the effect of temporarily paying down the publicly held debt during the years of Social Security surpluses and then borrowing the money back during the deficit years after 2017. The effect would have been similar to putting the money in a savings account at a bank during the surplus years and then gradually withdrawing it during the deficit years when it was needed to supplement the inadequate payroll tax revenue. .

If this had been done, Social Security would not even be in the news today. When Social Security surpluses end and deficits begin in 2017, the Social Security trustees would simply gradually sell the marketable Treasury bonds in the open market in order to raise money to supplement the inadequate payroll tax revenue. There would be sufficient Social Security money to pay full benefits until at least 2041 when the youngest of the baby boomers would be 77 years old.

The most important point to keep in mind when trying to understand all the confusing misinformation that is being put out by both sides in the debate is that there would be no Social Security problem whatsoever until at least 2041 if the Social Security surplus money had been saved and invested as envisioned by those who supported the 1983 "fix."

Major fraud, which I believe can be accurately referred to as a crime against the American people by their government, has been taking place for the past 22 years, and it continues on a daily basis.   President George H.W. Bush, President Clinton, and President George W. Bush, along with the majority of the members of Congress, have been parties to this crime.

They have gotten by with it, and continue to get by with it, because of the extreme economic illiteracy in America.   Few American have ever had even an introductory course in economics, and this includes most members of Congress.   The economics of Social Security funding is somewhat complicated, so few Americans really try to understand the basic facts.   They either align themselves with President Bush and his fellow conservatives who say that Social Security is in deep financial trouble, or they align themselves with the AARP and Democrats who argue that Social Security doesn't need to be fixed because "it's not broken."

I have followed the federal budget closely for nearly 30 years, and I have been deeply immersed in researching Social Security funding for the past five years.   This is my third book on the subject, and I believe I understand the big picture fairly well.

The American people are being bombarded with so many lies about Social Security from both sides of the debate that they do not know what to believe.   Sadly, there are partisan motives behind the deception coming from both sides, and the outcome of the debate may well be decided by which side is able to spend the most money in their effort to convince the public that they are right and the other side is wrong.

The one thing I can say with certainty is that none of the most vocal parties in this national debate are being totally truthful with the American people. If they were being honest, they would all agree that Social Security has some problems, but these problems could be fixed relatively easily.

The real problem that we should all be focusing on is the reckless fiscal policies that have led the nation to the brink of national bankruptcy. Social Security is one of the many victims of this reckless policy. Sufficient payroll taxes have been levied to keep the Social Security system sound and solvent for at least another three or four decades without any action being taken if the government had saved and invested that money. Unfortunately, the government has already spent $1.7 trillion of that Social Security revenue and continues to spend every dollar of Social Security surplus that flows in.

The government needs to stop spending the Social Security surplus revenue and repay the money that it has already spent. This would take care of the problem until at least 2041 when the real actuarial imbalance shows up. That problem can be solved by removing the cap on earnings subject to the payroll tax.

Currently everyone pays the payroll tax on all their earnings up to $90,000, and all earnings above $90,000 are exempt from the tax. I favor totally eliminating the cap so that everyone would pay Social Security payroll taxes on all of their income just as they pay income taxes on all income. Those people earning more than $90,000 received major tax breaks from Bush's income tax cuts, which were financed primarily with surplus Social Security revenue.

What the American people need to be told by their leaders is that, if the spent Social Security money is replaced and invested in marketable Treasury bonds or other real assets, if all future Social Security surplus revenue is saved and invested, and if the actuarial imbalance is corrected by removing the earnings cap, Social Security will remain solvent indefinitely.

	HOW THE GOVERNMENT EMBEZZLED THE SOCIAL SECURITY SURPLUS GENERATED BY THE 1983 PAYROLL TAX INCREASE
	What Was Supposed to Happen to the Surplus Revenue Generated by 1983 Social Security Tax Increase
Investment	The funds were supposed to be invested in pre-existing marketable Treasury bonds in order to pay down the publicly-held debt, dollar for dollar, with Social Security surpluses. Since current law required that the money be invested in government securities, the closest thing to putting it in the bank was to use the money to pay down the public debt during the surplus years and then borrow the money back when it was needed beginning in 2017.
Long-term Effect	If this practice had been followed, the publicly held debt would now be lower by $1.7 trillion, and interest earned on the investment would have been reinvested in additional marketable Treasury bonds held by the public. The federal government would have spent $1.7 trillion less unless they had raised taxes to fund additional spending or borrowed additional amounts from the public.
Asset Value	If the money had been invested in marketable Treasury bonds, the bonds could have been sold in the open market, without any additional government action, to raise funds to supplement the inadequate payroll tax revenue. The fund would be truly capable of paying full benefits until 2041.
Interest Received on Investment	Actual interest payments would have been made which would have been invested in additional marketable Treasury bonds.

	What Actually Happened to the Surplus Revenue Generated by the 1983 Social Security Tax Increase
Investment	The funds were not invested in any real assets. Instead, the government treated the revenue from the payroll tax increase as if it were new spending authority. The government used every dollar to fund other spending programs and tax cuts, and not a dollar was paid down on the public debt.
Long-term Effect	The government spent $1.7 trillion more than it could have spent without the existence of the Social Security surplus. The public debt is now $1.7 trillion higher than it would have been if the government had not had access to the Social Security money, unless the government had borrowed similar amounts form the public
Asset Value	The $1.7 trillion of non-marketable special-issue IOUs which the trust fund holds have no value until and unless the government at some point in the future decides to repay the money it has "borrowed." The special issues IOUs cannot be sold at any price. Beginning in 2017, when the Social Security trust fund will start running annual deficits, full Social Security benefits cannot be paid unless the government chooses to begin paying back the money it owes to the Social Security trust fund.
Interest Received on Investment	The Social Security trust fund has not received a dime in real interest payments. The trust fund "interest payments" are in the form of more of the non-marketable special issue government IOUs just like the ones the trust fund already holds. The surplus Social Security revenue has not been invested in anything. It has just been spent by the government and replaced with non-marketable government IOUs that are the equivalent of a note that a bank robber might leave in the vault stating how much money he has taken.

ACKNOWLEDGMENTS

Thanks to the many readers of my previous book, *The Looting of Social Security,* who have joined the crusade to save Social Security. A special thanks to Jerry Grusell and Dominique Tardif of Idaho and to Robert and Virginia Graf of West Virginia for their exceptional efforts to spread the message. I also want to thank the many readers who have taken the time to send me emails or call me with words of encouragement.

I am grateful to Carroll and Graf Publishers for allowing me to reprint some material in this book that first appeared in *The Looting of Social Security.* I am thankful for my special friend, Victor Stoltzfus, President Emeritus of Goshen College, for his encouragement and inspiration.

Most of all, I thank my loving wife, Joan, for her inspiration, encouragement, and support. Joan read every page of the manuscript from the first draft to the final one, and the book is much better because of her efforts.

INDEX

ADDENDUM

The Case for Universal Economic Education

This book describes how political leaders have managed to knowingly and deliberately inflict great harm on the economy, the federal budget, and the American people over the past two decades by pursuing policies that were incompatible with sound principles of economics.

The massive tax cuts pushed through Congress by President George W. Bush in 2001 and 2003 came on the heels of the first two deficit-free years that the nation had experienced during the past 40 years. The federal government was just beginning to get its head above the sea of red ink in which it had been drowning for so long when Bush shoved Uncle Sam's head deep into the sea of red ink again.

The problem is not that Bush cut taxes. Tax cuts can be positive or negative depending upon the circumstances. The problem is that Bush cut taxes without also cutting spending. It is that Bush lied to the American people about the true status of the federal budget. He said the government was receiving more tax revenue than it needed and that he was simply giving back to the taxpayers some of the excess money. He assured the American people that there would be no return to deficits and that none of the Social Security money would be spent on other government programs.

Economists were shocked at this outrageous economic malpractice. Approximately 400 of the nation's top economists, including 10 who had won the Nobel prize in economics, were so concerned about the damage the tax cuts would do that they took out a full-page ad in the *New York Times* in an effort to get their message to the public.

My first book, *Understanding Inflation and Unemployment*, which was published in 1976, was written because of my frustration with President Lyndon B. Johnson's failure to follow sound economic policies to head off the terrible inflation that was set off at least partly by the massive increase in spending on Vietnam without a corresponding increase in taxes. That book marked the beginning of my long crusade for economic education to combat the incredibly dangerous economic illiteracy of the American people.

Economic malpractice is possible only because of the high degree of economic illiteracy in America. Most Americans have never had even an introductory course in basic principles of economics, and this includes many members of Congress. Only a small percentage of American high school students receive instruction in economics, and even the majority of college graduates are economically illiterate, having made it through college without taking a single course in economics.

The best insurance we can buy against future economic malpractice is to reduce economic illiteracy. I urge readers to support universal economics education at the high school level, and to try to persuade colleges and universities to make principles of economics a general education requirement so that at least college graduates will be able to play a role in battling economic malpractice.

HOW TO CONTACT THE AUTHOR

Allen W. Smith has appeared on CNBC, CNN, CNNfn, and more than 150 radio talk shows. He is available for public speaking engagements, media interviews, and consulting.

Dr. Smith invites readers to visit his website at www.allenwsmith.com. to learn more about his ongoing crusade to save Social Security, and his efforts to reduce economic illiteracy. Excerpts from Dr. Smith's previous books are available for downloading at no charge.

In addition to writing books, Smith also writes inspirational/philosophical essays that are posted on his website. He invites readers to download free copies of the essays for personal use.

Dr. Allen W. Smith may be contacted by email or regular mail at the addresses listed below.

Email:
ironwoodas@aol.com

Mailing Address:
Allen W. Smith
P.O. Box 1397
Winter Haven, FL 33882-1397

Website:
www.allenwsmith.com